THE LITTLE BOOK OF
RUGBY

RUGBY'S A to Z

Written by Paul Morgan and Adam Hathaway

THE LITTLE BOOK OF
RUGBY

This edition first published in the UK in 2004
By Green Umbrella.

© Green Umbrella Publishing 2005
www.greenumbrella.co.uk

Publishers Jules Gammond and Tim Exell

Printed and bound in China

ISBN 0 9544561 5 7

Contents

Australia

FOR A COMPARATIVELY SMALL nation, Australia has a staggering record of sporting success in pursuits staged anywhere from the swimming pool and athletics track to the rugby ground and cricket pitch.

This pre-eminence is put down to many factors, most notably the healthy outdoor lifestyle enjoyed by Australian youngsters and their famous refusal to bend in the competitive arena. Whether the game is dominoes down the local or a World Cup final, Australians always want to win.

Their success in rugby union is remarkable. They are the only country to have won the World Cup twice (in 1991 and 1999) and with the wind in the right direction they may have made it three wins out of a possible five when losing to England in the 2003 final. Bear in mind that rugby union in most states of Australia is not the first-choice winter sport of many, coming second, third or fourth to rugby league, Aussie Rules and more recently the ubiquitous soccer. Thus, their success is even more admirable or envy-inducing depending on which side of the equator you come from.

However the love of the 15-man code down under was in evidence when they staged the most recent World Cup. Over two million paying spectators turned up to watch a tournament that stretched the length and breadth of the country, and even 'non-union' states embraced the event.

formation of the New South Wales and Queensland Rugby Unions in 1881 and 1892 respectively.

Seven years later, Australia played their first Test match when representatives of these unions teamed up to take on a touring side from the British Isles. The Australians marked their debut in international rugby with a 13-3 win in Sydney but lost the remaining three Tests to go down 3-1 in the series. In 1904, when the British returned, the visitors won all three Tests in the series. Then, in 1908, the 'Wallabies' were born.

The Australians toured the United Kingdom and North America and as they followed the New Zealand tourists, who were dubbed the 'All Blacks', it was, according to the Australian Rugby Union, suggested by members of the press that they should be called the

The first Australian rugby club was at Sydney University, formed in 1864, and in 1874 there were enough teams in the area to form a competition. Thus the Southern RFU was established, though it was run from Twickenham until the

OPPOSITE Australia's fans watch the action unfold during the 2003 Rugby World Cup Final

BELOW Australia's first ever international match vs the Lions, 1899

'Rabbits'. The team rejected this as the rabbit was an imported pest, so they settled on being named after the native wallaby instead.

They were no rabbits on the field however and the Wallabies won 32 of 38 games on that trip. They also took an Olympic gold medal back home after beating England, represented by Cornwall, 32-3 in the final in London. The effect of the First World War and the increased influence of rugby league saw union go backwards for a few years up to 1928 when the Queensland Rugby Union started up again.

In 1929, Australia beat New Zealand in all three Tests for the first time. They also adopted green and gold as their

BELOW Mark Ella, star of the Wallaby 1984 Grand Slam touring side

official colours and in 1934 they won the Bledisloe Cup for the first time, beating their old rivals New Zealand 25-11 in the first Test in Sydney and drawing the second 3-3.

After the Second World War, the Wallabies embarked on a triumphant tour of the United Kingdom and America. Considering the modern infatuation with defence, it is interesting to note that in four Tests against the home unions the Australian line was not crossed once. At the end of the trip, Australia were invited to join the International Rugby Board. They have hardly looked back since and their teams have thrilled spectators the world over.

In 1979, they won the Bledisloe Cup for the first time since 1949 and in 1981 Mark, Gary and Glen Ella became the first three brothers to be picked for the same Wallaby squad. Fly-half Mark was the star of the show and scored a try in each Test of the Wallabies' Grand Slam tour of the United Kingdom in 1984, repeating his achievement of 1977-78 when he toured the British Isles with the Australian Schoolboys' side.

He retired at the ridiculously early age of 25, but is still considered one of the finest No 10s ever to lace up a pair of

LEFT Nick Farr-Jones holds up the Webb-Ellis trophy after victory in 1991 over England

boots. The 1984 tour was a vindication of the Australian board's policy of reviewing their coaching philosophy after a lean time in the early 1970s.

The first Rugby World Cup took place, unfortunately without Mark Ella, in 1987 and was hosted in Australia and New Zealand as those two countries had

ABOVE The great John Eales' career ended on a high after Australia beat the 2001 Lions

They made amends in the next tournament in 1991 which was spread over the British Isles and France. In the semi-final in Dublin, the brilliant Australian wing David Campese scored one try and made another for centre Tim Horan to put New Zealand to the sword 16-6 and set up a Twickenham finale against England.

Campese did not get a chance to shine in a poor final, but the Wallabies were canny, and defensively sound, enough to win 12-6 and captain Nick Farr-Jones lifted the trophy to the grey London skies.

In 1999, Australia were easily the best side in the competition, winning the final 35-12 against France and providing a fitting international farewell for Horan, his long-time midfield partner Jason Little and flanker David Wilson.

The core of the side survived to defeat the British Lions 2-1 in 2001 and send the legendary second row and captain John Eales into retirement a happy man.

They narrowly missed out on victory in the 2003 World Cup final when beaten by a last minute Jonny Wilkinson drop goal, but they are sure to be punching their weight when the rugby world converges on France in 2007.

floated the idea of a global showpiece tournament in the first place.

The Wallabies made serene progress to the semi-finals and looked set for a place against New Zealand, the eventual winners, in the final. However, fate, or more accurately the French full-back Serge Blanco, intervened with one of the most famous tries in rugby history and the Australians lost a pulsating semi-final 30-24.

Barbarians

LEFT The 1973 Barbarians pose before their famous match against New Zealand

ONE TEAM SUMS UP THE ROMANCE and spirit of rugby union. Those famous men in their black and white hoops - the Barbarians!

The Barbarians, who are a United Nations of Rugby, represent a glorious concept. They embody the spirit of rugby, brought to life by the vision and enthusiasm of one man, William Percy Carpmael.

Invitations to play are sent to players from all corners of the rugby world as long as they adhere to the Barbarians motto: "Rugby football is a game for gentleman in all classes but never for a bad sportsman in any class."

ABOVE Gareth Edwards is chaired off the pitch after the 1973 victory

Inspired by his personal playing experiences with both Blackheath and Cambridge University, Carpmael's dream was to spread good fellowship amongst all rugby football players. The dream became reality on December 27th 1890 at Friary Field, Hartlepool.

In 1890, after the rugby season had finished in March, Carpmael took the Southern Nomads - mainly composed of players from Blackheath - on a tour to the north. As legend has it, in a restaurant in Bradford, the concept was agreed upon over supper. He saw the team as an opportunity to play with friends from various clubs who were normally opponents.

He loved the culture behind the rugby tour and came up with the idea of regular short tours involving players of the highest skill levels.

In Carpmael's vision this side needed no ground, clubhouse or subscription and membership was by invitation only, but that hasn't stopped them becoming one of the most revered sporting institutions in the world.

They are a scratch side, with players from all over the world, wearing the famous black and white hoops, black shorts, and their own socks, to exemplify the nations and clubs involved.

The only criteria a player must fulfill to receive an invitation from the Barbarians is: that the player's rugby is of a good standard and that they behave themselves on and off the field. "There is no discrimination on the basis of a player's race colour or creed," the club explain, "and since 1890, players from 23 different countries have worn the jersey.

Once invited a player becomes a life member of the club."

Winning and losing are never the most important things in a Barbarians match, as it is definitely a case of how you played the game, with flair and an eye not on the scoreboard but the try line.

Every rugby supporter, no matter which side they follow tends to be a supporter of the Barbarians and they have an incredibly successful Friends organisation and a website: www.barbarianfc.co.uk.

As a result of many scintillating performances, the Barbarians won respect worldwide and on January 31st 1948 they were invited to play the Australians at Cardiff Arms Park in the final match of that tour. It was their first against international opposition. The battle captured the imagination of millions

BELOW Jeremy Guscott playing for the Barbarians against England at Twickenham in 2001

and drew a capacity crowd of 45,000.

So successful was the fixture that it became tradition for Australia, New Zealand or South Africa - whichever was touring the UK - to tackle the Barbarians in 'The Final Challenge.'

Those great matches against touring sides hit a high point, in 1973, when the Barbarians took on New Zealand, at Cardiff Arms Park. On that day Gareth Edwards finished off a length of the field move, to score one of the most famous tries in the history of the game. THAT try went through seven pairs of hands, encapsulating everything about Barbarians rugby. An equally acclaimed victory was achieved in 1961 when the Barbarians played the South African Springboks captained by Avril Malan. The Springboks were unbeaten on their tour of Great Britain and Ireland.

In their last match of the tour the Barbarians held on to a 6 - 0 lead thanks to some fierce tackling and carried off the Springbok head - a trophy traditionally presented by the South African tourists to the first side to beat them when on tour.

Hundreds of internationals have represented the Barbarians but the most prolific was AJF (Tony) O'Reilly, the

Lions and Ireland wing, who made his debut as a Barbarian in 1955, helping the club to a 6-3 win against Cardiff. He went on to represent the club a record 30 times, scoring a record 38 tries, making his final appearance against Swansea eight years later in 1963.

When the game turned professional in 1995 it did threaten the existence of the Barbarians. They have lost many of their traditional fixtures against club sides. However, with great players like Jonah Lomu, Zinzan Brooke and Agustin Pichot backing the club and the presence of its spiritual leader, and president, Mickey Steele-Bodger never far away they now have a huge, and respected, presence in the world game.

Today the Barbarians hold such an important place in our game that other countries, like New Zealand, France, South Africa and Australia have set up their own Barbarians side, the New Zealand version coming to Twickenham in December 2003 to take on the newly crowned world champions, England.

One of England's greatest players, Jeremy Guscott, ended his international career with the Barbarians in the summer of 2001 on one of their now regular summer tours against the best of Britain and Ireland.

"There was to one final hurrah (in my career)," Guscott recalls in his autobiography, "and what a crack it was.

"It was good fun meeting up with the boys, just like an old-fashioned tour where the social side is as important as the playing side.

"I wish the Baa-Baas had had these tours before. I know it would have been nigh on impossible because of the way the game was structured and because the boys had day jobs, but it was one hell of an experience, one hell of a way to finish off."

Rather than allow professionalism to kill off the Barbarians the grand old club feeds off tradition and the desire of players and supporters to hold on to just one part of the amateur game.

Wilson Whineray described this great old club the best when he said: "Barbarian rugby is all about a feeling, spirit, essence to the game."

In 2004 the Barbarians embarked on another of their highly successful end of season tours of Britain, playing England, Scotland and Wales, as all three sides prepared for their summer tours to the southern hemisphere.

Calcutta Cup

SCOTLAND AND ENGLAND ARE the oldest rivals in international rugby having played their first Test match in 1871 at Raeburn Place in Edinburgh - a game that ended in victory to the Scots by a goal and a try to a goal.

Nowadays, the winning captain, in the annual fixture played during the Six Nations, receives the Calcutta Cup, an ornate trophy made from melted-down silver Indian rupees that has a history almost as interesting as the fixture itself.

On Christmas Day in 1872, a game of rugby was played in Calcutta between a 20-man side representing England and 20 men of Scotland, Ireland and Wales. This led to the formation of the Calcutta Football Club a year later.

However, the club was reluctantly disbanded in 1878 due to a lack of opposition and the 13 rupees that were left in the kitty were used to make a trophy

that stands 18 inches high, has three cobras as handles and an elephant on top. The cup was then donated to the Rugby Football Union to be played for by England and Scotland each year.

The first Calcutta Cup match in 1879 ended in a 3-3 draw but England took possession of the trophy when they won

in Manchester a year later. A tradition was born and over the years the match has thrown up some of the greatest rugby seen on the international stage as well as its share of controversy on and off the pitch.

Nothing is guaranteed to get the Scots up for a match more than squaring up to the 'Auld Enemy' and England have returned from Murrayfield with a bloody nose on more than one occasion - notably in 1990 and 2000 when they headed north in search of European Grand Slams only to pass back over Hadrian's Wall with their tails between their legs.

ABOVE Clive Woodwood calls the shots for England during their 1980 Grand Slam season

It was the Scots who were the first to be left red-faced, though, when they were so confident of winning in 1897 that they neglected to take the trophy with them to Manchester. Sport has a habit of bringing sides down to earth and England, led by Ernest Taylor, ran out 12-3 victors.

In 1925, Murrayfield staged its first ever international, fittingly a Calcutta Cup fixture, and the Scots used the occasion to claim their first ever Grand Slam. They ground out a 14-11 win to complete a clean sweep after victories over Ireland (14-8), Wales (24-14) and France (25-4). They did not repeat the feat for another 59 years.

In 1980, England travelled to Murrayfield looking for a Slam of their own. Captained by second row Bill Beaumont they had a centre in their side called plain Mr Clive Woodward - whatever happened to him?

Beaumont's side were clear favourites and duly did the business, winning 30-18 with winger John Carleton scoring a hat-trick of tries. The next time the red rosers ventured north in search of a Grand Slam it all panned out rather differently in 1990.

England, led by Will Carling, were perceived to be haughty and arrogant and everyone bar the Scotland fans had ignored the fact that David Sole's side were chasing a Slam of their own. The build-up to the match was dominated by talk of how it would be pay-back time for the English for the imposition of the unloved poll tax by Margaret Thatcher's government. Sole set the tone for the afternoon with his long, slow march on to the pitch at the head of his team.

Scotland took an early lead before being pegged back by a Jeremy Guscott try just before the break. Then Tony Stanger delivered the killer blow for the Scots in the second half beating the defence to touch down. England lost their heads completely, were rattled by the Scots and ended up arguing amongst themselves. Craig Chalmers' boot did the rest and to the strains of 'Flower of Scotland' from the crowd the hosts won 13-7, took their third Grand Slam and cross-border bragging rights for the next year. Sole said afterwards: "We were going for the same prize but in the English media it was as if it wasn't even a contest."

Not all of the most famous Calcutta Cup stories occur on the pitch and in 1988 the after-match celebrations made front and back page news. It's a good job there was something to talk about because the match itself was a desperate 9-6 win for England. Scottish flanker John Jeffrey and England No 8 Dean Richards livened up the Monday morning papers when it was disclosed that

BELOW Back Row England players, (L-R) Lawrence Dallaglio, Chris Jones and Richard Hill pose with the Calcutta Cup trophy after England's 43-3 destruction of Scotland at Murrayfield, 2004

ABOVE The Scotland players celebrate their 2000 Calcutta Cup victory

Blacks under their belt but were soon under the cosh when Rob Wainwright dashed through to score. England were reliant on the boot of Jon Callard for their points but looked to be sunk when Gregor Townsend dropped a goal in the 79th minute. However in injury time Callard knocked over a penalty, England breathed a sigh of relief and Scottish captain Gavin Hastings broke down in tears when interviewed on television.

Six years on, the boot was on the other foot. It must be cocking a snoot at the English that does something to the Scottish psyche because they demolished their visitors' Grand Slam hopes again in the Calcutta Cup match of 2000 at Murrayfield. England were again well-fancied and were cruising after Lawrence Dallaglio went over to score.

However the rains came, England failed to adapt and Duncan Hodge scored all of Scotland's points in a memorable 19-13 win.

If you are ever tempted to have a bet on a Calcutta Cup match, having weighed up all the form and are approaching the bookmaker's counter, remember the shocks over the years and do yourself a favour. Keep your money in your pocket.

they had over-indulged in the post-match hospitality and reportedly had an impromptu game of football with the Calcutta Cup through the streets of Edinburgh in the early hours. The cup was renamed the 'Calcutta Plate' by the tabloids, both players were severely disciplined and a Scottish silversmith repaired the damage.

Back on the pitch in 1994 the Scots had an agonising near-miss in the fixture losing 15-14 in Edinburgh. Carling's England arrived in the Scottish capital with a win over the All

Dragons

OF THE FOUR HOME UNIONS, Wales have arguably the strongest rugby heritage. The old cliché was that if they wanted a fly-half all the selectors had to do was whistle down a mine-shaft and the next Barry John, Phil Bennett or Jonathan Davies would emerge into the sunlight with coal dust in his eyes. He would then start goal-kicking the opposition to death whilst the fans gave a lusty rendition of 'Bread of Heaven'.

As well as providing great players, the Welsh have also provided some superb administrators, notably the late Vernon Pugh who was chairman of both the Welsh Rugby Union and the International Rugby Board.

While heading up the IRB, Pugh saw its membership double, helped set up the European Cup in 1996, served as a director of Rugby World Cup and was the driving force behind Italy's admission to the Six Nations.

They may never have won the World Cup but it is only in recent years that the Welsh public have taken a shine to the other football game, whereas in the rest of the six nations, soccer, Gaelic football and other winter pursuits have all enjoyed prominence.

It is no coincidence that the recent upsurge in the popularity of soccer in Wales came at a time when the rugby team was at its lowest ebb for a long time. But two performances in the 2003 World Cup - against New Zealand and England - and some decent displays in the 2004 Six Nations have given Wales's long-suffering and ever-optimistic fans the hope that their national team is on the up.

ABOVE Barry John kicks on during Wales' 1972 game against France at Cardiff Arms Park

To understand how Welsh rugby operates, however, takes some lateral thinking. When the New Zealander Steve Hansen announced his intention to resign as coach at the end of the 2004 international season, the Welsh Rugby Union narrowed the choice of his successor down to two men - the highly respected Llanelli coach Gareth Jenkins and the Mr Fixit of Harlequins, Mark Evans. Both had their supporters, so the WRU duly gave the job to Mike Ruddock who had previously ruled himself out of the race. The Welsh press had a field day as the non-runner won the Welsh National and Ruddock now has to carry a bigger weight than any racehorse - that of Welsh sporting history - on his shoulders.

Wales played their first international in 1881 against England and were on the wrong end of such a drubbing they refused to play the next year. After that fit of pique, the game in the Principality developed thanks to the efforts of manager Richard Mullock who was to become the first secretary of the WRU.

Mullock helped turn the Welsh into the most feared team on the planet. Their domestic club scene was strong and in the first 11 years of the 20th Century Wales won the international championship seven times - they even turned over the touring 'Invincibles' from New Zealand in 1905.

In the 1920s, though, Welsh rugby went downhill as the recession saw many potential players leave the country in search of work elsewhere while many more travelled to the north of England to play rugby league and earn a living from their talents. In the 1930s, the shoots of a Welsh recovery sprouted when they beat England at Twickenham for the first time and narrowly lost to the All Blacks.

Grand Slams were claimed in 1950 and 1952 before both Cardiff and the

BELOW The 1906 Welsh side that tied the Five Nations with Ireland

Welsh side beat the New Zealanders a year later. Finally in the late 1960s it all fell into place.

It is hardly a coincidence that in 1967 the great Gareth Edwards made his debut at scrum-half against France and a year later Wales appointed their first national coach, David Nash.

The 1970s were a golden period. Players such as Edwards, John, Bennett, John Dawes, JPR Williams, Gerald Davies and Mervyn Davies bestrode the rugby world and contributed hugely to two historic British Lions wins, over New Zealand in 1971 and South Africa in 1974.

The utter dominance of Wales over their neighbours during the 1970s can be summed up in three Grand Slams, five Triple Crowns and, just for good measure, a couple of wins over the Wallabies.

Although Wales were still churning out the talent in the 1980s, much of it was heading north to league, most notably Jonathan Davies, Terry Holmes and Rob Ackerman. The team of the 1970s had disbanded and, although they managed third place in the inaugural World Cup in 1987 and a Five Nations championship in 1994, the Welsh bandwagon hit the buffers. During the early

ABOVE The Welsh Grand Slam winning side of 1950

to mid-1990s, the likes of Allan Bateman, Scott Quinnell and Scott Gibbs moved to rugby league, thus weakening further an already limited pool of talent available to the Welsh selectors. Ironically, they all returned to the Welsh game when union turned professional after the 1995 World Cup.

In 1998, the WRU took the radical step of appointing a foreigner as national coach in the shape of New Zealander Graham Henry. The Kiwi was almost immediately dubbed 'The Great Redeemer' thanks to 10-match unbeaten run which included a dramatic 32-31 win at Wembley which denied England a Grand Slam.

Wales were playing their home games at Wembley at the time because

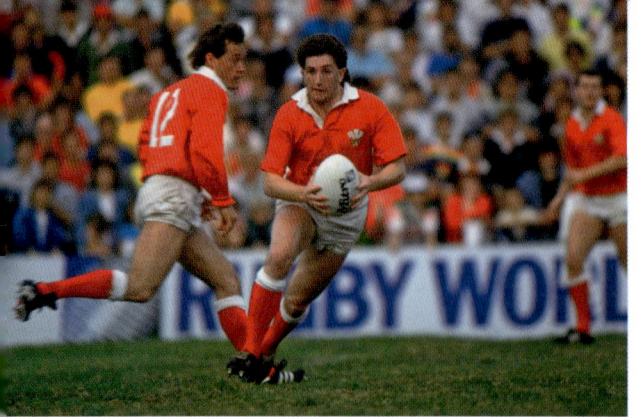

the magnificent Millennium Stadium in Cardiff was under construction as the Welsh prepared to host the 1999 World Cup.

The stadium was ready - just - for the tournament that Wales opened with a 23-18 victory over Argentina at their new ground. However, they went out at the quarter-final stage to the eventual winners Australia.

Henry resigned in February 2002 after a 50-point thumping by Ireland and was succeeded by his countryman Hansen. Hansen's record was nothing to write home about by the time he returned home in 2004 but he had overseen a radical period of restructuring in the Welsh game.

Taking their lead from the Irish domestic game, Wales formed five provinces to play in the Celtic League and Heineken Cup. Two sides, Llanelli and Cardiff, retained their identity while the other top clubs merged to form the Celtic Warriors (Bridgend and Pontypridd), the Dragons (Ebbw Vale and Newport) and the Neath-Swansea Ospreys.

The idea was to concentrate the best players in the five centres of excellence and raise the playing standards of domestic rugby in Wales. It is early days as far as this experiment is concerned, but there are signs that the Welsh are heading in the right direction.

England

WHEN JONNY WILKINSON'S DROP goal sailed through the Sydney posts in November 2003 to land England their first World Cup, it was the culmination of one of the most professionally painstaking campaigns ever put together by an English sporting side. It was also the complete opposite of the way the Rugby Football Union started in 1871.

Then, on 26 January, 21 English clubs met at the Pall Mall Restaurant near Trafalgar Square, to form a ruling body. There should have been representatives from 22 teams, but the man from Wasps went to the wrong watering hole, stayed there and missed the meeting. Some harsh critics of the authorities may say this absent-mindedness was a taste of things to come.

England played in the first ever rugby international, against Scotland in March

1871, and enjoyed success in the International Championship from its formation in 1883 to the mid-1890s.

However, there was trouble in the air and the disagreement between the RFU and its northern members over compensation for loss of earnings for players led to the split in 1895 that led to the formation of the Northern

ABOVE The Scotland and England teams that took part in the first ever international in 1871

ABOVE Eric Evans, captain of England's 1957 Grand Slam winning side

OPPOSITE Bill Beaumont playing against Scotland in 1980, England's Grand Slam year

Union - which would become the Rugby League. English rugby union lost a lot of players to the new code and would not regain the International Championship until 1910, the year when England played Tests at Twickenham for the first time.

By the time of the 1924 Calcutta Cup match, the ground held 43,000 spectators and its development was matched by that of the England side which played some of its best rugby during the period. Despite losing many players in the First World War when the RFU urged all of its men to sign up for action, the English won the Grand Slam in 1921, 1923, 1924 and 1928. They would not win another for 29 years until Eric Evans led his side to a clean sweep.

After Evans's success in 1957, it was a further 23 years before England, led by Bill Beaumont and boasting players such as Fran Cotton, Clive Woodward and Roger Uttley, won the Slam again in 1980.

The years between the Evans and Beaumont successes were particularly barren for the English. They did not win

in Cardiff between 1963 and 1991 – even though they had talented enough players they did not produce the goods on the pitch.

There were highlights, though. John Pullin's 1972 tourists beat South Africa away and a year later the hooker led his team to victory over the All Blacks in Auckland. These glitches apart, the period was marked by selectorial incompetence. In 1979 the North, watched by the chairman of the English selectors Budge Rogers, beat the touring

New Zealanders 21-9 at Otley. Running the show from fly-half was Alan Old (the brother of the English Test cricketer Chris). But rather than play Old in the Test match the week after, the selectors picked Les Cusworth and broke up the North's back row. New Zealand were there for the taking but England missed their chance.

Mike Davis's appointment as England coach heralded a revival that ended in Beaumont's team winning the Grand Slam, but it was only as the 1990s approached that England began to punch their weight and make the most of their huge playing resources.

In 1988 Will Carling was made England captain, starting his reign with a win over Australia at Twickenham and became one of the most recognisable sporting faces in England.

When England blew the Grand Slam against Scotland in 1990, in a match notable for the squabbling among many

of the England players, Carling's leadership was questioned. He answered the critics by leading England to Slams in 1991, 1992 and 1995, and taking them to the 1991 World Cup final.

Carling also led England at the 1995 World Cup in South Africa where they were knocked out in the semi-finals by the incredible hulking form of Jonah Lomu. Carling himself nearly did not get that far. Before the tournament he was quoted as saying the RFU was run by '57 old farts'. The quote was apparently meant to be off the record, but it was too good for the makers of a documentary to leave out of the trailers for

ABOVE Will Carling's first game as England captain, a 28-19 victory over Australia 1988

ABOVE & OPPOSITE
2003 was meteoric for England winning both the Grand Slam and Rugby World Cup

the programme. Carling was sacked but the players threatened not to play for anyone else so the RFU reinstated the skipper after he had apologised. Carling was captain until 1996 when he stepped down after leading England to 44 wins from 59 games in charge.

Clive Woodward became England coach in 1997 and two years later he urged everyone to "judge me on the World Cup" after a series of indifferent results. England were drop-kicked out of the tournament by South African fly-half Jannie de Beer in the quarter-final in Paris, but Woodward survived to continue his revolution within English rugby.

Martin Johnson, who had captained the victorious 1997 Lions, was Woodward's captain after Lawrence Dallaglio was forced to resign following allegations of drug-taking in a Sunday tabloid. The road to the 2003 World Cup in Australia was littered with history-making results as England set about laying almost all of their bogeys, but the journey was far from smooth.

In November 2000, fresh from a last-minute win over Australia, the England players went on strike over money. The players were unhappy that their match fees were not guaranteed but included a win bonus. Woodward was incandescent and expelled the players from the team hotel, saying he would play himself against Argentina the following Saturday if the players did not see sense. Eventually, the situation was sorted out and the team beat Argentina and South Africa in successive weeks.

Woodward's side had several Grand Slam flops but were gathering momentum. They supplied the bulk of the 2001 Lions squad, beat the southern-hemisphere teams regularly at Twickenham and destroyed Ireland to claim their first Slam in 2003.

Away wins against New Zealand and Australia followed and ensured England went into the World Cup back in Australia as the world's top team. They spluttered once or twice during the tournament, but Johnson would not be denied the crowning glory of his brilliant career. His retirement, and Wilkinson's absence while recovering from a shoulder operation, were contributory factors to England's disappointing Six Nations campaign in 2004.

France

FRANCE REPRESENT TWO EXTREMES to the rugby fan. On their day they can beat anyone in a style to gladden the hearts of the purist, but on an off-day they can be a complete shambles. In the 1999 World Cup semi-final against New Zealand, they turned round a 24-10 deficit to win 43-31 in a contest billed by some pundits as the greatest game ever played. In the final against Australia a week later, they barely turned up and John Eales, the Wallaby captain, threatened to take his side off the pitch in protest at the rough-house tactics of the French.

Rugby was introduced to France by a group of English merchants who formed Le Havre Athletic Club. The club still exists though, shamefully, they play soccer now. None the less they have retained their original colours of light and dark blue that were representative of Oxford and Cambridge universities.

The first French championship was held in 1892, with the Racing Club de France beating Stade Français, though the 'STADISTES' got their revenge the following year in a repeat of the final. The game spread swiftly through France with a Scotsman taking it to Bordeaux and a Welshman forming a club in Bayonnne. Soon the entire south of the country was converted.

France won the Olympic gold medal for rugby in 1900, beating Germany in the final, but the Federation Francaise

handed response from the IRB to the way rugby was run in France, with players reputedly being paid to play and crowd trouble breaking out at some games. Twelve French clubs split from their federation and their 14-13 win over England was the last championship game for the French for 16 years. They eventually settled their differences with the IRB and were readmitted after the Second World War.

Rugby in France made great strides in the years after the war and in 1958, led by Lucien Mias, they won a series in South Africa for the first time. But their rows with the authorities rumbled on - they were accused of choosing rugby league

ABOVE France take on England in Paris in the 1958 Five Nations

OPPOSITE The French team celebrate after their amazing 43-31 1999 RWC semi-final victory over New Zealand

de Rugby was not formed until 1920. Before the birth of the FFR, the national team were busy but not successful - in 28 internationals before the First World War they won just once, shocking Scotland in 1911.

In 1920, the French won their first international away from home, beating the Irish, and gave England a scare at Twickenham. But their improvement was stalled in February 1931 when the IRB announced that all French fixtures would be abandoned at the end of that season. Their suspension was a high-

'Monsieur Drop' and named at fly-half in the French XV of the 20th Century when it was announced at the turn of the millennium.

The late 1960s and early 1970s were a golden period for the French. They won the Five Nations in 1967 and 1968 and shared the title in 1970 and 1973. During this time, their biggest rivals in European rugby were the Welsh and the two countries shared some epic battles. Jo Maso, now the French team manager, was one of the stars of the show along with Guy Camberabero, Claude Dourthe and Pierre Villepreux.

In the 1980s, France were consistently the best side in Europe and won Grand Slams in 1981 and 1987 under the coaching of Jacques Fouroux. Philippe Sella, who won 111 caps at centre, hooker Daniel Dubroca and the peerless full-back Serge Blanco were the mainstays of the side with Blanco proving himself one of the most exciting runners the game has ever seen.

Blanco scored perhaps the most dramatic try of all time to earn France a place in the 1987 World Cup final. Playing Australia in Sydney in the semifinal, the French were behind three times in the match but still snatched an

players by Scotland in 1953, and they were not accepted as official members of the International Board until 1978.

The French shared the championship in 1954 and 1955 before winning the tournament outright in 1959, 1961 and 1962. From 1961 to 1963, the top scorer in the competition was the French full-back-turned-fly-half Pierre Albaladejo - arguably the first superstar of the Gallic game. Albaladejo was the first Frenchman to land three drop goals in an international when he scored a hat-trick in the 23-6 win over Ireland in 1960. He was given the nickname incredible win. David Campese and David Codey scored for Australia and Michael Lynagh's boot kept the favourites in front. Alain Lorieux, Sella and Patrice Lagisquet all crossed for tries but the Aussies led 24-21 as injury time approached. Didier Camberabero levelled the scores with a penalty before Blanco intervened.

From deep in their own half, France ran the ball through 11 pairs of hands before Blanco charged at the line and scored in the corner to silence the Australian crowd. They could not repeat the magic in the final and lost to the All Blacks. The next two World Cups were disappointing and in 1999 they were runners-up again after their magical afternoon at Twickenham against New Zealand in the semi-final.

In Europe, the French were vying with England for 'top dog' status and won back-to-back Grand Slams in 1997 and 1998. After the 1999 World Cup, coach Jean-Claude Skrela was replaced by Bernard Laporte. Laporte took them to a Slam in 2002 but their 2003 World Cup campaign ended in disappointment.

The French were the form team of the tournament going into the semi-final against England and were strongly fan-

cied to see off Clive Woodward's side who had spluttered in getting the better of Samoa and Wales in particular. As they made the journey to Sydney's Telstra Stadium, the heavens opened and all the French confidence and swagger disappeared as the rain fell.

Fly-half Frederic Michalak was overshadowed by his opposite number Jonny Wilkinson as England's forwards played the conditions perfectly and the Woodward's men ran out

BELOW Serge Blanco celebrates his magnificent try in the RWC semi-final against Australia

comfortable winners.

France and Laporte got their revenge at the first time of asking in the 2004 Six Nations when they rounded off a Grand Slam by beating England in Paris, a match they looked like winning in a canter until the world champions upped their game in the second half. But France held on to win 24-21 and lend weight to the theory that they and not the world champions are still the best side in Europe.

BELOW The French team celebrate their 2004 Grand Slam after victory over England

Grounds

RUGBY UNION IS BLESSED WITH so many magnificent stadiums, some the most impressive in their respective countries. But the ground that sets the benchmark in the game is the home of English rugby, **Twickenham**.

The Twickenham Stadium - which also housed home games of the Harlequins - made its debut in 1909 when the Quins took on local rivals Richmond, and won 14-10.

A year later the England team ended their nomadic existence and were running out at Twickenham, to beat Wales 11-6, in a season when they won the Championship.

To establish the new home of English rugby RFU treasurer, William Cail, paid £5,573 for a cabbage field at Twickenham, which had been discovered by a committee member, Billy Williams.

ABOVE The magnificent Twickenham Stadium

Now that same cabbage patch is being transformed again into a stadium with a wraparound roof, 83,000 seats, an in-house hotel, health club and leisure centre, which the RFU hope will be ready for 2007.

Television cameras moved into Twickenham for the first time in 1938. The great old stadium even survived being bombed in the Second World War, and 46 years after the end of the War staged the final of the second Rugby World Cup.

If Twickenham sets the benchmark there is one ground, across the Severn

velopment of Wembley host to every major English Football Association cup final. Its facilities ensured FA Community Shield of 2001 between Manchester United and Liverpool became the first football match played under a closed roof in the UK. It has also been the venue for a number of major pop concerts.

With construction work still going on the stadium hosted its first rugby game in 1999 and saw Wales record a victory over South Africa, Mark Taylor having the honour of scoring the opening try at the new venue.

Crowds of around 70,000 regularly pack into Twickenham and the Millennium Stadium, especially for Six Nations games but the ground that still holds the record for the championship is Scotland's **Murrayfield**.

Bridge, which is a great pretender to their crown, **The Millennium Stadium**.

Built in 1999 for the Rugby World Cup, The Millennium Stadium was built on the site of one of the most famous sports venues in the world – The National Stadium, at Cardiff Arms Park.

The Millennium Stadium was a magnificent backdrop to the 1999 World Cup and provided a sensational venue for the final between Australia and France.

International rugby had been played on the site, in Cardiff, since 1884, the former stadium, Cardiff Arms Park, became one of the most famous.

Since the new stadium opened it has also been home to cricket, speedway, the Wales football team and with the rede-

Scotland may not have fared well on the pitch in the 1950s but they did break one record. More than 80,000 people came to Murrayfield (a world record for a rugby match at the time) to watch the Scots hammer Wales 19-0 in 1951. Swelling the crowd, and to show that some things never change, there were 25,000 Welshmen in the ground!

Not content with that, and although Scotland failed to win a Championship outright during the 1970s, they did play their part in one world record. On St David's Day 1975 104,000 people flooded into Murrayfield to see the Scots beat Wales 12-10.

Twickenham, The Millennium Stadium and Murrayfield are modern all-seater stadiums but the one ground in the Six Nations with the most character, and often the best atmosphere is Dublin's **Lansdowne Road**.

The world's oldest rugby ground was opened in 1878, hosting its first international in the same year, against England. The 49,000-capacity ground is situated just over a mile south of O'Connell Street in Dublin.

Lansdowne Road may be the oldest but in France they have one of the newest in the rugby world, in the

ABOVE The atmospheric Lansdowne Road

80,000-seat **Stade de France**. Built for the 1998 Football World Cup it has developed into one of the most atmospheric grounds in the world, and was certainly the noisiest in the 2004 RBS Six Nations.

A £250milllion state of the art stadium on the outskirts of Paris it has taken over as France's home ground from the world famous Parc des Princes which could hold 30,000 less fans.

Joining the Millennium Stadium, in opening in 1999 was **Stadium Australia**, which four years later was the centerpiece of the Rugby World Cup. The site of a former abattoir, ten miles west of Sydney, it set the world record

ABOVE Stadium Australia hosting the 2003 Rugby World Cup Final

OPPOSITE Eden Park, Auckland, hosting a Super 12 game

for attendance at a rugby match when 108,878 came to see New Zealand against Australia, in 2000.

That day Jonah Lomu took centre stage as the All Blacks won 39-35 at the venue, which was built to house the 2000 Sydney Olympics.

Stadium Australia isn't the only stunning stadium in the Southern Hemisphere and although those in neighbouring New Zealand aren't as big, their names are steeped in the very history of rugby.

Eden Park in Auckland is perhaps the most famous in the land of the long white cloud.

It has been in existence as a sports ground since the year 1900. It became the home of Auckland Cricket in 1910

and the home of Auckland Rugby in 1925 after the Union had leased the grounds since 1914.

Eden Park, which is a very open arena and unlike many other in the rugby world, hosted the first World Cup final, in 1987. It has been used for Test rugby since 1921. Its current capacity for rugby is 45,472 and 42,000 for cricket.

On New Zealand's south island the Test venue in Dunedin is the famous **Carisbrook** ground. The 33,000 capacity home to the Otago Highlanders Carisbrook was transferred to the Otago Rugby Football Union in June 1907 and, in 1981, the ORFU bought the freehold

ABOVE Ellis Park, Johannesburg

land title from the Presbyterian Church.

In South Africa there are some sensational rugby stadiums but one stands out above all others - the scene of the 1995 World Cup final - **Ellis Park**.

First opened in 1928 after the Transvaal rugby union negotiated for the site with a Mr JD Ellis the ground has become synonymous with South African rugby.

The stadium, which now holds 80,000 was redeveloped at a cost of £60 million, the new Ellis Park rising in 1982, the bill boosted by many problems along the way.

Ellis Park was also the scene when South Africa re-entered international rugby in 1992 with a Test match against New Zealand.

Today Ellis Park is the home ground of the Lions, the Cats, Kaizer Chiefs Football Club and is also the premier concert venue in South Africa.

Eden Park, Carisbrook and Ellis Park have been the scene of a number of sensational 15-a-side encounters but for classic Sevens there's only once place to go, **The Hong Kong Stadium**.

The ground may not be the biggest in the world, holding 40,000 people, but it has been important in the development of the game, bringing it to new audiences.

In the So Kon Po valley this impressive stadium was built in 1994, a gift from the Hong Kong Jockey Club to the island.

Heineken Cup

ONE OF THE BIGGEST SUCCESSES of professional rugby, in Europe, the Heineken (European) Cup was launched in 1995. It was started under the initiative of the then Five Nations Committee. They were looking for a new level of cross-border competition to bridge the gap between a country's domestic league and international matches.

The Super 10 (and then Super 12) was the forerunner of the Heineken Cup. In the Southern Hemisphere the Super 12 received universal acceptance from the off, but the Heineken Cup kicked off with 12 teams from Ireland, France, Wales, Italy and Romania, with Scotland and England absent.

The first match took place in Romania with Farul Constanta losing to the eventual first champions Toulouse, 10-35. The English and Scottish sides didn't stay out in the cold for long, and a year later the revamped Heineken Cup kicked off with 20 teams in four pools.

The main difference between the Super 12 and the Heineken is the composition of teams.

All the sides in the Super 12 represent provinces while in the Heineken Cup there is a mixture of provinces, club and district sides. The Irish teams

represent their provinces, like Munster, Leinster and Ulster, while in England it is club sides like Leicester, Bath and Northampton.

The diversity of the sides and the history that accompanies so many of them brings a breadth and tradition to the competition that no other can match.

But before those giants of the English game arrived Toulouse emerged as the first champions, winning a final 21-18 at the National Stadium in Wales, against Cardiff.

Without the English sides the first tournament failed to capture the imagination of the European rugby public and just 21,800 spectators watched that first final. Although from then on the tournament grew and grew.

Any doubts about the future of the tournament were ended in the following season. The resolve of the organising committee was proved correct with Scottish and English sides confirming the Heineken Cup as a truly pan-European tournament, already bridging the gap between domestic and international rugby.

The arrival of the English and Scottish teams in the 1996-97 season put paid to the Romanians as they dropped out, although they re-emerged

ABOVE Brive captain Alain Penaud holds the Heineken European cup after beating Leicester in the 1997 final

OPPOSITE Toulouse and Cardiff played out the first ever Heineken European Cup final in 1996

in the second tier of the Heineken Cup, the European Shield.

With the Heineken Cup now embracing 20 teams, in 1996, the four pools were fiercely competitive. Only Leicester and Brive emerged from the pool stages unbeaten. Giants like Wasps, Leinster and Munster failed to make the quarter-finals.

Three English sides made the last eight with Leicester moving into the final, where they faced Brive in front of 41,664 fans, again at the National Stadium in Wales. Significantly the final was watched by almost double the number of supporters as 12 months earlier. A live TV audience also brought the

final to 35 million viewers in 86 countries. The Heineken Cup had arrived with a bang!

The 1997 final failed to go Leicester's way, Brive winning 28-9.

Around 350,000 spectators had watched matches in 1996-97. But by the time the 1997-98 final arrived this had leapt to almost half a million, confirming that the Heineken Cup had captured the imagination of the rugby public.

This 1998 final will go down in history as one of the most dramatic, Bath and their travelling army of supporters beating holders Brive at a packed Stade Lescure Stadium in Bordeaux, 19-18.

"That was a day of drama and no little emotion, especially for an ex-Bath man" recalled Sky Sports commentator and former England outside-half Stuart Barnes.

"We left the ground and knew a great sporting tournament was up and running. Few would argue that rugby union has found itself a special as the best of Europe crosses borders to provide action, atmosphere, the whole panacea."

Derek McGrath chief of the organisers, ERC adds: "The tournament continues to go from strength to strength. Fundamental to the growth of the

BELOW Jubilant Bath fans after their victory in '98

Heineken Cup had been the rising standard of professional club and provincial rugby across Europe, ensuring an even more exciting future for the tournament."

A row between Heineken Cup organisers, ERC, and the English clubs led to a boycott by the latter of the 1998-99 tournament. This ensured that Bath were unable to defend their crown they won, the 16 remaining teams taking part in four pools of four.

Many felt the absence of the English sides would lead to a French domination but it was an Irish side, Ulster, that upset the odds to win it.

French clubs filled top spot in three of the groups. But Ulster beat Toulouse (twice) and reigning French champions Stade Francais on their way to a Dublin final against Colomiers, who they beat 21-6

A capacity Lansdowne Road crowd of 49,000 watched Ulster win, along with a worldwide television audience estimated at over 36 million.

The new decade saw the start of an English domination of the Heineken Cup with the first three finals of the new Millennium being won by top English sides.

LEFT Simon Mason of Ulster kicks for goal against Colomiers '99

BELOW (left to right) Ben Cohen, Tim Rodber and Pat Lam of Northampton lift the trophy after the 2000 Heineken Cup Final against Munster

ABOVE Austin Healey makes a try saving tackle on Munster's John O'Neill during the 2002 Heineken Cup Final

Once one Midlands side had won it, it was left to another one, Leicester, to take a firm grip on the trophy. The Tigers became the first side to win it twice and they managed it in back-to-back years.

The losing finalists of 1997, Leicester took their first Heineken Cup in 2001, beating Stade Francais in their home town of Paris, in a sensational final, 34-30.

More sold out signs went up for this final, Leicester outscoring the Paris club three tries to none. Centre Leon Lloyd scored two and flanker Neil Back one so they could walk off with the massive trophy.

Leicester's second title came in Cardiff, in 2002, when they beat Munster in front of a tournament record 74,000 crowd, 15-9. Tries from Geordan Murphy and Austin Healey and the illegal intervention of Neil Back at a scrum, knocking the ball out of Munster scrum-half Peter Stringer's hand, taking Leicester home.

The eighth Heineken Cup final, in 2003, broke more new ground, as it was the first all-French affair. Toulouse beating Perpignan 22-17, to become the second side to win Europe's premier tournament twice.

The 1999-2000 tournament set a new record when for the first time four different nations - England, Ireland, France and Wales - made it through to the semi-finals.

But it was the English side (Northampton) and the Irish (Munster) who turned up at Twickenham in front of a record crowd of 68,441, as Northampton won 9-8.

Ireland

WITH SPORTS LIKE GAELIC FOOTBALL, hurling and soccer taking so much of the attention in Ireland, the rugby union side has one of the smallest player bases amongst the major unions. Compared to England's 200,000 players Ireland have just 11,500, across 200 clubs. But that hasn't stopped them pulling off some sensational results in their history including, in 2004, England's first defeat at Twickenham for more than four years.

The game originated in Ireland around 1850, probably started by former pupils of Rugby School and Cheltenham College, who played the game at Trinity College, Dublin.

Ireland played their first international, against England, in 1875 at Kennington Oval and this was beginning of a tough opening period for the Irish. After losing that first game to England, comprehensively, they had to

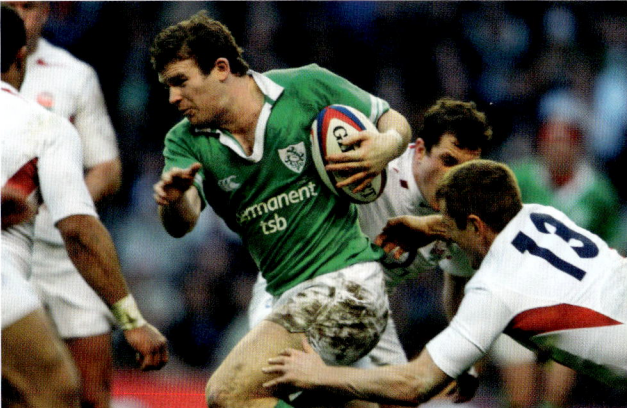

wait six years for their first win, a victory over Scotland.

That first international side had nine from Dublin University and six from the North of Ireland, demonstrating a unique mixture.

Today the national side is almost exclusively made up of players from their four provinces Munster, Leinster, Ulster and Connacht, three from the south and one from the north of Ireland.

Throughout history, despite the political troubles between the north and the south, the Ireland rugby team has always been selected from players from both sides of the border.

ABOVE Gordon D'Arcy, player of the tournament in the 2004 Six Nations

ABOVE Irish Grand Slam hero Jackie Kyle

Irish politics did affect rugby in the 1970s, the 1972 season becoming a non-event in Championship terms. Due to the troubles in Ireland both of their home games were cancelled and Wales, playing three games only ended unbeaten and on top of the table. Ireland with only two games to their name were also unbeaten.

Unbeaten runs for Ireland were rare in the early years. Although they did pick up Triple Crowns (victories over England, Wales and Scotland in one season) in 1894 and 1899 their overall record in the Championship is worse than any other of the sides, bar Italy.

England, Scotland and Wales all won Grand Slams (victories over all the other nations in one season) in the early years of the Five Nations but Ireland had to wait until after the Second World War for their first clean sweep.

Despite having some great teams in the last century, the Irish side have only managed to deliver one Grand Slam to their long-suffering fans, in 1948.

The Irish road to the Grand Slam had begun a year earlier with the first Five Nations Championship since the War. The title was shared between Wales and England but already the Irish were starting to show the green shoots of recovery and to build a formidable side.

A capacity 32,000 crowd packed into Ravenhill to see Ireland clinch their first Grand Slam with a 6-3 victory over Wales. Outside-half Jackie Kyle and hooker Karl Mullen were two of their greatest heroes. This Ireland side scored ten tries in their four games, a better record than for the 20 years before.

Crucially Ireland had built a magnificent back row for that Grand Slam year in Des O'Brien, Bill McKay and Jim McCarthy. Kyle - the genius at fly-half – was for many people one of the greatest players ever to play rugby union.

"I think the ability to remain error-free at crucial moments was a notable characteristic of the Irish side of that period. Then we had Kyle, in my view incomparable before and since," said Mullen in Edmund Van Nesbeck's Irish Rugby Scrapbook.

"I know that many people think we had just one back of quality, in Kyle, but I do not agree at all. Kyle was the genius and the inspiration, but in defensive terms I think our backs were first class and our centres on that day (against Wales), Paddy Reid and Des McKee, were brilliant in defence. We had scoring power on the wings too."

LEFT Ireland scrum-half John Moloney races clear to score a crucial try in Ireland's 26-21 victory over England at Twickenham, 1974

BELOW Michael Kiernan, so often the kicking hero for Ireland

A Triple Crown followed Ireland's 1948 Grand Slam, a year later, but they had to wait until the 1970s and 1980s for more glory.

Ireland won the Championship in 1974, and they had Mike Gibson - who scored two tries against England - ruling the roost in the backs. And a certain legend, called Willie John McBride in the pack. (See M for McBride).

Twenty one points from Ollie Campbell for Ireland against Scotland at Lansdowne Road delivered a rare Triple Crown in 1982. Three years later the Irish came closer still to the Five

Nations' ultimate prize. This time they were thwarted by a bruising 15-15 draw with the French, in Dublin, but they still ended the season one point clear at the top.

Again the Irish looked to the boot, but this time it belonged to Michael Kiernan, who slotted five penalties from seven attempts, while the French scored two tries.

Ireland won the 1985 Triple Crown and the Championship in a 13-10 Dublin win over England. And again it was Kiernan who proved the hero dropping a vital, injury time drop goal.

ABOVE The Irish team celebrate winning the 2004 Triple Crown by defeating Scotland

Nineteen long years passed until Ireland pulled off their next, remarkable Triple Crown, and second place in the Championship, in 2004.

The seeds for the 2004 Triple Crown were sown a year earlier when they lost just one game, the Grand Slam decider to England at Lansdowne Road.

It seems remarkable that Ireland could lose 42-6 in Dublin and a year later win 19-13 at Twickenham, a victory that set them on the road to their first Triple Crown since 1985.

That 2004 Triple Crown was finally clinched in a comprehensive victory over Scotland but it was effectively won at Twickenham, earlier in the Championship.

After the defeat, which was England's first at Twickenham for 22 matches Ireland captain, Brian O'Driscoll said: "To beat them at home and in their first competitive match at Twickenham as world champions makes this among the top three sweetest days of my career, if not the sweetest.

"We always knew it would be tough coming over here but we knew we were capable of beating any side in the world if we perform to the best of our ability."

Sandwiched between those two Six Nations matches against England was a 2003 World Cup campaign that was full of ifs and buts for the Irish.

They went out in the quarter-finals to a rampant French side but they had come within a David Humphreys drop goal of beating reigning champions Australia. Had Humphreys' late kick sailed over, rather than sailed wide Ireland would have faced a quarter-final against Scotland, and an almost guaranteed passage into the last four.

Their 2003 campaign although unfulfilled was far better than the one they staged in 1999, losing in the quarter-final play-offs to Argentina and having to face the ignominy of qualifying for the 2003 tournament.

Johnno, Jason and Jonny

CLIVE WOODWARD KNEW IN HIS heart of hearts that his England side that won the World Cup would never play again and his feelings were confirmed when captain and king of the rugby jungle Martin Johnson retired from international rugby prior to the 2004 Six Nations. The 114-times capped prop Jason Leonard won his final cap against Italy in that competition whilst Jonny Wilkinson was ruled out of the tournament with a neck injury.

Wilkinson is still a young man and should return to continue his assault on the record books, but Johnson and Leonard are gone forever from the international stage. Will we see their like again? It is doubtful. When Leonard bowed out, the trio had won precisely 250 caps between them and scored 832 points of which Wilkinson had contributed 817.

The older pair were the last of a dying breed in that they had actually tasted real life before becoming full-time rugby players when the game went professional in 1995. Leonard worked as a carpenter, once returning to his building site the day after an international to make up time lost at training, and Johnson was probably the world's most unlikely bank clerk. The thought of asking Johnson for a loan probably never crossed the minds of his opponents over the years who he gave precisely nothing bar a handshake once the game was over.

Johnson can legitimately lay claim to be the greatest player England has ever produced although he wouldn't do it himself. The records support this assertion. Three Lions tours, including two as captain, two Grand Slams, a World Cup, four Zurich Premierships, back-to-back Heineken Cups, 84 caps and two international tries.

He is the first to admit that his playing style was hardened by a stint in New Zealand as a teenager and no less a judge than Colin Meads wanted him as an All Black. But he made his England debut against France in 1993. He was flown out as a Lions replacement later in the year, went virtually straight into the Test team and was a first choice for England ever since.

Johnson won his first Grand Slam under Will Carling in 1995 and led the Lions to victory over South Africa in 1997. He was not national captain at the time but as manager Fran Cotton said: "We wanted someone who would knock on the opposition dressing room and intimidate them." He managed that, but his game was not just built on his undoubted hardness and he turned himself into the archetypal, all-purpose, multi-tasking modern lock in the last six years of his career. He was the best forward at the 2003 World Cup having tacked running and handling skills on to the historical basics of second-row play. He became England captain in 1999 and Woodward summed up his team talks when he related that all Johnson said in the dressing room was: 'Let's get on with it'. His men would follow him anywhere and he was sorely missed when he departed the international scene.

Leonard was in the trenches with Johnson for most of his international career which began in the intensely hostile environs of Buenos Aires in 1990. There are still English pressmen wandering around patting themselves on the back for predicting that the Barking lad would win a century of caps and 13 years later they were proved right when Leonard led the England team out against France. One press box veteran recalls that after the first scrum against the fearsome Argentinian pack in Leonard's debut international, he turned to a colleague and said "We've got one here". England certainly did have one and Leonard overtook Philippe Sella as the world's most capped player when he came on as a replacement against France in the 2003 World Cup semi-final.

To put his achievements into perspective, consider that Sella was a centre and rugby's other centurion, David Campese, was a winger. Leonard was a prop, could play equally well on either side of the scrum and underwent a career-threatening neck operation in 1992.

Leonard's versatility served him well as did his ability to adapt to the professional era. He is one of rugby's most sociable players and always sought out his opposite number for a pint after a game. But you don't get to a hundred caps by being in the bar all the time and Leonard knew there was a time and a place for everything.

Whilst Leonard and Johnson would not win any prizes in a beauty contest, Wilkinson had become the darling of the media even before dropping the goal that won the World Cup. Only Will Carling has enjoyed, or in Wilkinson's case endured, such a high profile, but he takes it all in his stride and refuses to let

LEFT 'How Much Longer?!' Jason Leonard looks up to the Gods in 2000

BELOW Rugby's three centurions – David Campese (left) Jason Leonard and Philippe Sella (right)

the demands of the insatiable British press impinge on the most important thing in his life, namely rugby.

BELOW Jonny Wilkinson kicks for stardom

Wilkinson was first capped as an 18-year-old replacement against Ireland in 1998 and has hardly been out of the team since. Wilkinson - the world's best goalkicker, probably pound-for-pound the best tackler on the planet and continually improving his running game - is the real deal. His first start in an England shirt did not go totally to plan as he was on the wrong end of a 76-0 beating from Australia in Brisbane on the infamous 'Tour of Hell' in June 1998.

In the following year's World Cup, Northampton's Paul Grayson was preferred as England went out to South Africa in the quarter-finals in Paris, but Wilkinson was back in the side for the 2000 Six Nations and the subsequent summer tour when he masterminded a second Test victory over the Springboks which triggered England's period of domination over the southern hemisphere's Big Three.

After helping England secure the Grand Slam in 2003, Wilkinson was the subject of intense scrutiny at that year's World Cup, not least by the Australian press who were clearly running scared of England's peerless match winner.

His immaculate goal kicking kept England in the tournament when they were misfiring and saw off the French in the semi-final. Before extra-time in the final, Woodward was trying to get a tactical message to Wilkinson but the fly-half insisted he had to go off and practise his kicking. Ever the professional, he must have the same scriptwriter that Ian Botham employed in his pomp because, inevitably, it was a Wilkinson drop goal that won the Cup, his kick that sparked celebrations not seen in England since the triumph in that other World Cup in 1966.

It propelled Wilkinson on to the front, middle and back pages, but has not affected him one iota.

Kickers

THROUGHOUT RUGBY'S HISTORY there are countless examples of when the boot was mightier than the sword. Kicks have been winning games since the days when William Webb Ellis was supposed to have picked up the ball. Two World Cup finals have been decided by late drop goals so the role of the kicker can never be over-estimated and every great team has had a player who is deadly with the boot. In this chapter we look at the four most successful goal-kickers in the history of the game.

1. NEIL JENKINS
Wales/Lions – Test points: 1090
IF you had to place your last penny on a man to kick a penalty you wouldn't go far wrong with the man they called the Ginger Monster, Neil Jenkins.

The outside-half from Church Village ended his career with an incredible 1049

ABOVE The most famous kick in the history of rugby!

LEFT Neil Jenkins in 2001, the year he surpassed 1000 points in Test matches

points for Wales (41 for the Lions) to his name, from 87 Tests, more than 200 better than his nearest rival.

His record is all the more remarkable if you consider he played for a Wales team that struggled in the 1990s and he was subjected to comparisons with the legendary No 10s who he followed into the famous red shirt.

There's no question that Jenkins outlasted all his critics and became, in 2001, the first player to score 1000 points in Test matches.

"Whatever figures I end with will be overtaken at some time in the future, but the first player to reach 1,000 points holds that honour for eternity," said Jenkins.

He made his Wales debut in 1991 but for many rugby fans it will be his role in the 2001 Lions series win over South Africa where he is most fondly remembered.

Those Lions won a Test series in South Africa for the first time in 23 years and it was the ice cool kicking of Jenkins that regularly kept them on track.

The end of Jenkins' international career certainly wasn't the end of his goalkicking feats. In 2004, playing for the Celtic Warriors he converted a remarkable 44 consecutive kicks.

2. DIEGO DOMINGUEZ
Italy/Argentina – Test points: 1010
WHEN Italy were admitted to the Six Nations in 2000 it was in no small part to the influence of Diego Dominguez.

The Argentinean born fly-half made his debut in 1991 against France and from then until his final game in 2003 many of Italy's best performances revolved around him.

It is one thing to be kicking goals from every corner of the field when your side is winning, when your pack is on top and the pressure is not at its heighest. So in many ways, with Italy often on the back foot, the kicking record of Dominguez stands the test of time even more impressively than some of his rivals.

Dominguez changed allegiance to Italy after waiting behind Hugo Porta, in Argentina, for his chance in international rugby. A season in France and then another in Italy convinced him to move to the Azzurri, qualifying through the grandmother.

Dominguez was the lynchpin of three Italian World Cup campaigns, playing in the 1991, 1995 and 1999 tournaments.

His influence on the Italian team was best demonstrated by the reaction to his first retirement from international rugby in 2000. He was coaxed back by then coach Brad Johnstone and the hopes of the Italian nation, eventually giving way before the 2003 World Cup.

Dominguez has played for the French club Stade Francais since 1997, helping them to the domestic championship a year later.

3. ANDREW MEHRTENS
New Zealand – Test points: 932

ONE of the finest outside-halves of his generation Andrew Mehrtens is the most prolific goalkicker in the history of New Zealand rugby.

Mehrtens made his All Blacks debut in 1995, playing in the World Cup final later in that season.

He overtook Grant Fox as the highest point-scorer in New Zealand Test history in 2000.

No-one has scored more penalties (181), drop goals (10) or conversions (162) than Mehrtens, who is also New Zealand's most capped outside-half. Mehrtens is the leading scorer in the Tri Nations, with 309 points in the annual competition.

A proud Canterbury Crusader Mehrtens was an integral part of their incredible run of three consecutive Super 12 titles, which started in 1998.

Mehrtens toured Europe with the All Blacks in 2002 but was one of the high profile absentees from John Mitchell's

OPPOSITE Diego Dominguez playing for Stade Francais

BELOW Andrew Mehrtens lines up another for the All Blacks

2003 World Cup squad. However the All Blacks failed to find a dependable goal-kicker to take his place and significantly he signed a new one-year contract with the New Zealand Rugby Union in 2003.

At the 2003 World Cup All Blacks legend Sean Fitzpatrick said: "The British continue to be amazed that Andrew Mehrtens - undoubtedly the best kicker in the game alongside (Jonny) Wilkinson - is not with the All Blacks in Australia."

4. MICHAEL LYNAGH
Australia – Test points: 911
WHEN Neil Jenkins went to the top of the international kicking league in 1999 it was by overtaking the record of the remarkable Michael Lynagh.

The Queensland outside-half was part of the sensational Australian side of the mid-1980s that went on to lift the Rugby World Cup, at Twickenham in 1991.

Lynagh made his debut for Australia in 1984 announcing his abilities to the world on the Wallabies' Grand Slam tour of Britain and Ireland later that year.

ABOVE Michael Lynagh burst onto the British scene in Australia's 1984 Grand Slam tour

The Australians were desperate for a man to fill the boots of the legendary Mark Ella and in Lynagh – who played centre in 1984 - they found a player that was more than up to the task.

Lynagh overtook Andy Irvine as the world's leading scorer at the 1987 World Cup, accumulating 72 caps and 911 points in his career, captaining the Wallabies 15 times.

Goalkicking wasn't the only area in which Lynagh broke records. Lynagh at No 10 and Nick Farr-Jones at No 9 lined-up together for the Wallabies, 47 times between 1985 and 1992, more than any other half-backs in the history of the game.

England's win over Australia in the quarter-finals of the 1995 World Cup was Lynagh's last Test. Once he'd quit the international scene he moved to England to play for Saracens, before becoming a television pundit.

Lynagh's Wallaby coach Bob Dwyer said of him: "Michael is very controlled as a person and possesses tremendous composure. I cannot remember an occasion when I saw him panic. As a player he also had tremendous running skills and width of vision, not to mention his obvious kicking ability."

Lions

THE LIONS REPRESENT THE ENDUR-ing fascination of rugby. They are fact for a while and then they become legends. There is no other side like them in the world because they compete at the very pinnacle of the game for a short, breathless time, and are then consigned to history.

It has always been like that. The Lions started life as the British Isles Rugby Union Tourists back in 1924 and, although they are more accurately described these days as the British and Irish Lions, the pattern of their operation is unchanged.

They now play major Test series, with other supporting games, in Australia, New Zealand and South Africa every four years. The squad is put together, meets its commitments and then breaks up. Only extremely rarely would the Lions play anywhere other than in the Southern Hemisphere.

The tours these days are extremely demanding. Once, the Lions would play 25 games or so on the road but in response to today's demands on players they face no more than a dozen matches, including three Tests, on their ventures.

ABOVE Dr Ronald Cove-Smith with the ship's captain en route to Cape Town with the 1924 Lions

"I went to South Africa with the '55 Lions and we were there for four months," remembers the great Welsh fly-half Cliff Morgan. "We had time to take in so much around the tour as well as play the matches."

Modern communications have brought the Lions into the homes of their key fans thousands of miles away. In 1974, for example, when the Lions won a Test series in South Africa for the first time, TV viewers in Britain did not see the action until three days later.

Now, all Lions' games are televised live wherever they are. "When I went on the 1938 tour to South Africa there were no journalists from home with us," said the late Vivian Jenkins, the former Wales full-back.

It was obvious from the start of the Lions' existence that winning a Test series anywhere in the Southern Hemisphere was a demanding business. That made it all the more rewarding when they claimed even a single Test victory – they took one in New Zealand in 1930 and another in South Africa in 1938.

After World War Two, the Lions did not return to business until 1950 with a 23-match tour of New Zealand. Next, the legend of the Lions acquired another significant chapter in 1955 when they shared the Test series with South Africa 2-2 and established all kinds of records, including a crowd of 95,000 for the first Test in Johannesburg. The Lions won that Test 23-22 with the South African Jack van der Schyff just failing to kick a goal in the last minute for victory.

The 1955 Lions woke up the world of rugby. They had set new benchmarks for the British and Irish game and everyone wanted more. All this fuelled

massive expectation for the 1959 tour to Australia and New Zealand (Australia had to wait another 30 years for the Lions to tour there exclusively).

Ronnie Dawson, the Ireland hooker, was tour captain and after the Lions had swept through Australia unbeaten, winning two Tests, New Zealand could not wait for them. More than 800,000 watched the 25 games played there. But there was scant reward for the Lions in international terms and their first Test defeat by 18-17, six penalties against four tries, is a bitter memory to this day. New Zealand won the first three Tests, the Lions the last.

Three more Lions' tours in the Sixties, two to South Africa, one to Australia and New Zealand, saw the

Southern Hemisphere remain on top, but the Seventies brought dramatic changes, beginning with the tour to Australia and New Zealand in 1971. The Lions knew they had an outstanding squad under the captaincy of the Welsh centre John Dawes, with another Welshman, Carwyn James, in charge of coaching.

But what made this tour stand out so strongly in the eyes of the world was the Welsh half-back pairing of Gareth Edwards and Barry John whose work behind a well-organised pack of forwards was mercurial. Edwards could

LEFT Ronnie Dawson, captain of the 1959 Lions Tour

BELOW "The King" Barry John was imperious during the 1971 tour of New Zealand

ABOVE Willie John McBride leads out Gareth Edwards and the rest of the 1974 Lions

OPPOSITE Lions Captain Martin Johnson and team mate Rob Henderson celebrate victory after the 1st Test against Australia

play for only 10 minutes in the first Test but John was in full command throughout and kicked two penalties as the Lions won 9-3.

New Zealand stormed back in the second Test, winning 22-12, but there was more than enough belief in the Lions' camp that they could take the series and they went on to do so with a 13-3 win in the third Test and a 14-14 draw in the last. John, who was one of 12 players to appear in all four Tests, scored 191 points in 17 matches and was given the nickname "King" during the tour.

The next mission, to South Africa, was only three years later and this time the captaincy was in the hands of the Ulsterman Willie John McBride, on his fifth Lions tour and very determined to take the battle to the very heart of the Springboks' strength - their powerful and match-hardened forwards. Again, the Lions depended on a hard core of 17 players who played in all four Tests and throughout the 22-match trip the Lions remained unbeaten.

The Lions rampaged through South African rugby, setting and raising standards match by match under McBride's cold-eyed leadership. They took the first Test 12-3, the second 28-9 and the series clincher at Port Elizabeth by 26-9. It was then something of an anticlimax when they were held to a draw in the final Test.

From this high point, the Lions were to fall behind once more. They lost in New Zealand in 1977, in South Africa in 1980 and in New Zealand again in 1983. And with the first Rugby World Cup to be played in 1987, there were some doubts whether the Lions would survive in the changing structure of the game.

But in 1989, on their first tour solely to Australia, the Lions, led by the

Scottish back-row forward Finlay Calder, brought their cause right back to the top of the agenda. Against an Australian squad, the bulk of whom were to capture the World Cup two years later, Calder and his men overturned defeat in the first Test to take the next two for the series, finishing in style in Sydney where they punished a glaring error by David Campese, the brilliant but opinionated Australian wing.

Four years later, under another Scot, Gavin Hastings, the Lions lost the series 2-1 in New Zealand. In 1997, with England's Martin Johnson at the helm, they stunned the South Africans by winning the most recent series there 2-1, winning the first two Tests to emphasise their strengths.

Thus, it was no surprise that the 2001 Lions under Johnson went to Australia as narrow favourites, followed by thousands of optimistic, red-shirted fans. That series was destined to go down to the wire and the Lions, after winning the opening Test in fine style, suffered the ultimate disappointment of losing the next two, the last by a margin of 29-23.

McBride and Meads

WILLIE JOHN McBRIDE AND COLIN Meads were born a world apart, McBride in Northern Ireland and Meads in the North Island of New Zealand. Yet because of rugby, these two icons of the game became the closest of rivals, the greatest of friends.

In his 55 Test matches for New Zealand, right in the heart of the All Blacks pack, Meads reckoned he played against McBride more times than any other opponent and regarded him as the greatest of competitors. According to Meads, they had "some rare old contests" and he respected McBride for his tenacity and his ability, adding that few packs would have had a more devoted and fired-up core man.

On opposite sides, Meads for New Zealand and McBride for the British and Irish Lions, their rivalry reached a peak in the 1971 Test series in New Zealand - which the Lions won. McBride still recalls putting his arm around Meads at the end of the final Test and thinking: "This is what I had dreamed of, beating the All Blacks on their own soil."

These two men came from totally different backgrounds but grew up to

Tests, and was captain of the unbeaten 1974 squad in South Africa. Ireland won the Five Nations' championship in 1974 under McBride's leadership.

Both men are of farming stock. McBride was one of six children, born in County Antrim. His father died when he was aged four and the family was brought up by his mother on a small farm. McBride's only club, from start to finish, was Ballymena and it was from their second row that he graduated to the Ireland side in 1962, winning his first cap against England.

He and two other great Irish players, full-back Tom Kiernan and centre Mike Gibson, were to be the backbone of the team for a decade.

McBride's farewell game in Dublin was in 1975 when he led a joint Ireland-Scotland team to victory over England-Wales in the Ireland centenary match by 17-10. At the start of the following season, he told the Ulster team that he no longer wished to be considered for them - and by definition his Ireland days were over as well. Eight years later, he coached Ireland for a season when the side failed to win a game.

Much as McBride was born, shaped and driven by Irish rugby at all of its

OPPOSITE Willie John McBride (left) and Colin Meads (right). Similar players.

dominate rugby at the highest level. Meads played 55 Tests for New Zealand between 1957 and 1971 while McBride played 63 Tests for Ireland between 1962 and 1975, 43 of them in succession which overtook the record set previously by the Scotland prop Hugh McLeod.

To underscore the statistical difference between the two men a little further, McBride made a record five tours with the British and Irish Lions, played in 17

ABOVE Willie John McBride takes on England in 1974, Ireland's Championship-winning year

is no greater honour for any sportsman than to represent his country," McBride said at the time. "To be selected for the Lions and don the famous red jersey was the special icing on a most enjoyable playing career."

When McBride captained the Lions in South Africa in 1974, his players still recall the incredible tension in the squad before they won the decisive third Test. They remember the final team meeting before they left for the ground and some believe not a word was said. McBride just looked each player in the eyes and then asked simply: "Men, are we ready?"

Colin Meads, the rangy hill-country farmer, was called Pine Tree from an early age. He was not a world figure in the way that many players are these days because there was nothing like the same exposure from television and other media for the game. But he was respected everywhere, and certainly feared by many throughout the game, and the longer he played the more his legend grew.

He farmed at the hamlet of Te Kuiti in King Country and he would work all day and then train in the evening for his next game. Meads was born for rugby -

levels, it was unquestionably in the red shirt of the Lions that he made his greatest impact on the world stage. There was no World Cup in those days, and meetings between the leading nations of the world were far fewer. As a result, tours by the Lions were eagerly awaited and played out before massive crowds.

In 1986, at Cardiff, the Lions made a rare appearance at home to play the rest of the world in a match to mark the centenary of the International Rugby Board.

"It has always been my view that there

he weighed 11 pounds at birth, one pound less than his brother Stan. He left school before his 15th birthday to begin his enduring relationship with farming and rugby.

On the other side of the world, Willie John McBride would join a bank in Ballymena, his only job.

Meads began his international career in 1957 against Australia in Sydney. He scored a try in his second match. In eight of his 15 years in the New Zealand side, the team was unbeaten. Match by match, his aura grew. But in 1967, playing against Scotland in Edinburgh, Meads was sent off for lunging at one of his opponents.

He was the first player to be sent off in an international for 42 years and his dismissal brought reactions and debate far beyond a straightforward international rugby match. It consumed New Zealand. One of the biggest names in world rugby had been dismissed and, to this day, there are people who are still prepared to debate the whys and wherefore of the incident.

McBride learned much from Meads, even if their playing contacts were limited. They were similar players in that neither was a classic line-out stylist. Of

ABOVE Colin 'Pine Tree' Meads in action against France in 1968

course, they could win the ball and win it well. What happened next demonstrated the sheer combativeness of both players.

Indeed the story is told of McBride and Meads in opposition for the first time, Ireland v New Zealand at Lansdowne Road in Dublin in 1963. McBride reminded Meads that he was around and Meads went down. Meads was then told by his captain Wilson Whineray to get up and make the next line-out. He did. Minutes later, McBride was down.

The two great men last competed against each other in Auckland in 1971, Meads as captain of New Zealand, McBride as a key forward for the Lions. That the Lions won that four-Test series is history but Meads has always believed that his team was in something of a dip and that the Lions, shamelessly copying

some aspects of New Zealand forward play, knew it and benefited from it.

Meads played on for two more years and bowed out in a match at Wellington where thousands bade him farewell.

McBride's own tribute was: "Colin was the best, most aggressive and, perhaps, the most totally committed player I ever played against."

BELOW Willie John takes on Colin Meads' Wellington during the 1971 Lions Tour

New Zealand

SINCE RUGBY KICKED OFF ITS international life at the end of the 19th century one side has set the benchmark. One side is feared throughout the rugby world. One side is the team to beat at every Rugby World Cup - the New Zealand All Blacks.

Rugby is the national sport in New Zealand. Everyone – men and women – seems to have played, everyone loves the game and everyone pays attention when the All Blacks are in town.

The first recorded game in New Zealand took place in May 1870; its introduction in the country credited to Charles John Monro.

The first fully representative team was the 1893 team that made the trip to New South Wales, captained by Tom Ellison. New Zealand played their first Test match in 1903, a victory over Australia, 22-3. Albert Asher scored their first try and the first points came from Billy Wallace.

Many things characterise the New Zealand All Blacks, setting them apart from most others, and one of those things is the challenge they set down to every team they face, with their haka.

Before every Test match the whole All Blacks side - usually led by a Maori player - take apart in the war dance in the centre of the pitch. An event to send chills down the spine.

NEW ZEALAND

The first time the haka was seen in the UK was during the 1888-89 tour. Then a side, made up mainly of Maoris, played an incredible 107 matches in 14 months, on a trip that took in both Australia and the UK.

No history of New Zealand rugby should ignore the debt the All Blacks hold to the Maori. They still have their own international side - but not Test recognised - and they have left an indelible mark on New Zealand, and world rugby.

In the early years of international rugby two New Zealand sides changed the face of the game.

The first in 1905 was known as The Originals. Captained by the legendary Dave Gallaher his team won all but one of an incredible 33-match tour, scoring 868 points and conceding just 47. The only defeat on the tour coming in controversial circumstances, against Wales, 3-0.

Following Gallaher's side, the 1924-5 All Blacks - The Invincibles - swept all

OPPOSITE Brian Lochore introduces his 1967 All Blacks to the Queen at Twickenham

before them beating Ireland 6-0, Wales 19-0 and England 17-11. In the 1920s, All Blacks like Bert Cooke, George Nepia, and Maurice and Cyril Brownlie were seen and never forgotten.

Historically New Zealand's fiercest opponents are South Africa. The Springboks first toured New Zealand in 1921, a drawn 1-1 series setting the tone for decades of hard-fought, colossal rugby. In that series the last Test was drawn 0-0 and in 1928 when New Zealand went to South Africa again

there was nothing to separate the teams. This time they tied the series 2-2.

The All Blacks have produced some of the best rugby in the game's history and in the 1950s they became the undisputed world champions.

In 1949 the All Blacks lost every one of the six Tests in which they played but from 1950 went on an incredible run, losing just five of their 24 internationals.

The 3-0 series victory over the Lions in 1950 started the renaissance and in 1956 New Zealand won a Test series against South Africa for the first time.

This time it was Don Clarke, or Superboots as he was known, who took control. They completed the 1956 series victory, 3-1, at Eden Park (see G for Grounds) with an 11-5 win. South Africa were defeated in a Test series for the first time - by any side - in 60 years. The All Blacks followed this up in 1959 with a 3-1 series victory over the Lions.

Feared the world over the 1967 team inspired the greatest run of consecutive wins in the history of All Black rugby. They went 17 Tests, from 1965 to 1969 without losing a single one. Brian Lochore's 1967 All Blacks are thought to be the finest New Zealand side of all time and when they arrived in the

In the 1970s the All Blacks had two almighty series with the Lions but when the 1978 team arrived in Europe records tumbled. Graham Mourie's 1978 All Blacks became the first to complete a Grand Slam in Britain and Ireland. They beat Wales 13-12, Ireland 10-6, England 16-6 and Scotland 18-9. The only side to beat them on their 18-match tour were Munster.

Outside of the Test scene members of the New Zealand rugby union regarded the domestic challenge competition, The Ranfurly Shield as important. But in the modern era they realised that it wasn't enough to provide competition for their domestic sides. So in 1976 they decided to form the National Provincial Championship, allowing all 27 unions to compete in three divisions.

British Isles, just one draw, against East Wales, prevented a perfect record.

Lochore was appointed New Zealand captain - for the 4-0 victory over the Lions in 1966 - following the retirement of Wilson Whineray. In those days the announcement of the new All Blacks captain ranked up there with the announcement of a new Prime Minister.

Without formal leagues in Britain until the 1980s the establishment of the NPC was ground-breaking. This fiercely-fought competition, helped New Zealand reach the top of the world game in the 1980s.

Considering New Zealand's position through rugby's history it was fitting that they lifted the first Rugby World Cup, in 1987 (see W for World Cup).

The 1987 side took the loss of its captain Andy Dalton in its stride before the tournament, immediately finding another great leader in David Kirk to take them into battle. From John Gallagher at full back to John Kirwan on the wing Kirk's side dominated the tournament. From the first game when they beat Italy 70-6, to the last where they overcame the impressive France side, 29-9, it was New Zealand all the way. The 20-point margin in the final was the closest any side got to beating the 1987 All Blacks.

New Zealand failed to repeat the win in 1991 and at the 2003 World Cup had to settle for their second successive exit at the semi-final stage.

At the 2003 World Cup they won back some pride with a third/fourth place play-off win over France but their semi-final exit to Australia still cost coach John Mitchell his job. Mitchell was soon replaced by former Lions and Wales coach Graham Henry. In 1995 helped by seven tries from the sensational Jonah Lomu they swept into the final, only to lose in extra time to South Africa.

They have always made it as far as the semi-finals but the ultimate prize has eluded them since that first tournament.

Oxford and Cambridge

THE SECOND TUESDAY IN DECEMBER when Oxford take on Cambridge in the Varsity Match at Twickenham is one of English rugby's great social occasions. The car parks at HQ are full of the hampers and champers brigade, determined to have a good day out as always, but on the pitch things have changed slightly over the years. With the onset of professionalism and the academies set up by the clubs around the country, you are less likely to spot a future international playing in this historic game than you were in the past. Fortunately, that does not deter thousands of spectators from turning up and having a huge pre-Christmas party.

It may be an anachronism in these days of eye coaches and nutritionists, but it is a good excuse for current students, past scholars and interested neutrals to let their hair down and have a few beers. The roll of honour is impressive with players such as Rob Andrew, Stuart Barnes, Gerald Davies, Chris Oti, Rob Wainwright and Gavin Hastings all playing in the game, as did BBC radio rugby commentator Ian Robertson in

1967. Robertson's colleague Alastair Hignell, who also went on to play for his country, scored a record 45 points in four Varsity Matches between 1974 and 1977. Three other famous names - Phil Horrocks-Taylor (1956), Gareth Rees (1994) and David Humphreys (1995) - each scored 'full houses' of a try, drop goal, conversion and penalty in Varsity games.

The first Varsity Match was played in February 1872 at 'the Parks' in Oxford after Cambridge initiated the fixture and it has been played every year ever since, barring the periods covered by the two World Wars. Oxford won the first match and Cambridge the second with the next two drawn, and the two sides were neck and neck until the 1990s when the light blues of Cambridge won a succession of matches. Of the 122 games played up to December 2003, Oxford had won 51 and Cambridge 57. There had been 14 draws, including the 2003 match that ended 11-11, but Cambridge did not take the lead in the series until 1981.

ABOVE Charlie Desmond of Cambridge scores the equalizing try during the 2003 Varsity Match

OPPOSITE Future Scotland and Lions star Rob Wainwright (centre) playing for Cambridge in the 1986 Varsity Match

In 1873 the match was played in Cambridge before it was decided to move it to the Kennington Oval and up until 1875, when the fixture was made 15-a-side, the teams fielded 20 players each. Several games were played at Queen's Club in Fulham before, in 1921, the match was moved to Twickenham.

In the early 1970s, the fixture was in the doldrums until an insurance company, Bowring, took over the sponsorship. The universities started to recruit more mature students with rugby pedigrees and the fixture recovered. It is now played in front of a near full-house every year for the MMC (Marsh and McLennan) Trophy. The firm had merged with Bowring in 1980.

Every player in the Varsity Match receives his blue (dark blue for Oxford and light blue for Cambridge), but rugby struggled initially to get Full Blue status. The Cambridge Rugby Club applied for the full status in 1883, but Reginald Gridley, the university boat club president, and the athletics and cricket clubs put up a host of objections to rugby being granted the same status as cricket and rowing. The president was apparently not impressed that thousands of people went to watch the Varsity rugby match and that the sides fielded international players. He decided that the rugby union and football clubs should share a number of full Blues between them.

The rugby and soccer sides disagreed with this and the next year they awarded themselves Blues, forcing the Boat Club to bring the dispute before the whole university in an open debate at the Union. A huge audience saw the Boat Club back down and finally agree to award Blues for rugby union and football.

There have been many bizarre and memorable games between the two great universities over the years. For instance in 1920 Oxford were captained by the South African Denoon Duncan who took the unusual step of selecting Boet Neser, a prop, at fly-half. The modern philosophy of a player not taking any notice of the number on his back and playing total rugby had been bought into even in those days! But confounding all expectations, Neser made the first try and scored the last. Unsurprisingly, the game is known as 'Neser's match'.

Recently, there have been murmurs that the universities are recruiting too many foreign players just to play in the match, but that is nothing new. In 1953, the Oxford side had nine overseas players, including seven from South Africa. That year's Dark Blue vintage were dubbed 'Springboxford'.

Aside from their day in the sun, or more usually driving rain, in December, the universities have contributed hugely to English rugby. William Webb Ellis, who supposedly 'picked up the ball and ran' in the first place, was a student at Brasenose College and the Oxford University Rugby Football Club was founded in 1869, about 15 months before the RFU, and is regarded as the oldest club in England.

Cambridge University Rugby Union Club was officially formed in 1872 and club officials helped to draw up the

BELOW A minute's silence is held in memory of Ian Tucker prior to the 1996 Varsity Match

inscribed on the monument and the Ian Tucker Foundation raises awareness of sports-related brain injuries.

The Varsity Match is not the be-all-and-end-all for either club, who have managed to maintain a high-quality fixture list despite the advent of professionalism and have games against the likes of Wasps, Leicester and the RAF.

And since the game turned professional, the universities have continued to supply international rugby players. The likes of Simon Moffat, Marco Rivaro, Mark Denney and Mark Robinson, for example, have all played at the highest level after a spell in Varsity rugby.

laws of rugby which were adopted by the RFU. It became a Constituent Body of the Union in 1872 and in 1896 started playing matches at the famous Grange Road.

Oxford's ground at Iffley Road is graced by the Ian Tucker Memorial Statue, a tribute to the player who died after being injured playing for the Dark Blues against Saracens in 1996. The names of the Best and Fairest player from the Blues XV each year are

Pienaar

IN EVERY GENERATION THERE ARE sportsmen who transcend the game changing it, on and off the pitch, forever. One such man was Jacobus 'Francois' Pienaar.

Pienaar, born in January 1967, was the man charged with the responsibility of taking South African rugby, not only out of isolation, but into a new era when they would host the third Rugby World Cup.

South African sport had been left in the wilderness for almost a decade. Banned from international competition because of worldwide opposition to their political system, Apartheid, which promoted a divided society, the Springboks were unable to play any official rugby Test matches.

So when they were re-admitted the game in the Republic needed not just a mere player, but a statesman and a role model for a new generation into the bargain. They got it with Pienaar.

One of the game's most enduring images is of Pienaar at the end of the 1995 Rugby World Cup, with the Webb Ellis Cup, alongside the country's new President Nelson Mandela, who was dressed in Pienaar's famous No 6 shirt. Pienaar was quite simply one of the most important figures in the history of rugby union.

ABOVE The most famous picture in rugby as Francois Pienaar accepts the 1995 RWC trophy from Nelson Mandela

South Africa's role in rugby union had been central since their first Test match in 1891 and so powerful were they as a rugby playing nation that it took England until 1969 to actually beat them.

So when the sporting boycott, because of the Apartheid regime, began to bite, it hit rugby union perhaps the hardest of all sports, as it removed one of the most powerful countries from the game.

That rugby boycott was in place in the late-1980s, ensuring that South Africa, who would have been one of the favourites, missed the first two World Cups in 1987 and 1991.

But after Apartheid was smashed and Nelson Mandela made his unforgettable

Walk to Freedom, in 1990, it was time to begin their re-integration back into the world of sport. When that ban was lifted in 1992, and they returned to international rugby it was always going to take great men and women to complete the country's integration back into international sport.

The International Rugby Board set the ball rolling by offering the new South Africa, the Rainbow Nation, the 1995 World Cup. It was then that Pienaar began to leave his indelible mark on the sport.

As the South African Springboks had been unable to play serious international rugby for almost a decade, Pienaar came into that World Cup as captain, with only 16 caps to his name. He galvanised not only a team but also a nation behind the men in green.

"Amongst sporting leaders, Francois Pienaar stands out. It was under his inspiring leadership that rugby, a sport previously associated with one sector of our population and with a particular brand of politics, became the pride of their entire country," the country's president, Mandela wrote in the book Rainbow Warrior.

"A beacon in our process of nation-

BELOW Hennie Muller leads his legendary Springbok side out to face Scotland in 1951. The Scots were thrashed 44-0

building will always remain the Springboks under his captaincy winning the World Cup in 1995.

"Seldom before or since has the country celebrated in such harmony and togetherness. Francois Pienaar's leadership extended way beyond the rugby field, and he truly represented all South Africans."

The thing that makes Pienaar stand head and shoulders above other rugby captains and coaches was the effect he had on the wider political world. He did so much to ease South Africa back into international sport after years on the sidelines due to Apartheid.

Due to this isolation Pienaar had a relatively short international career, playing just 29 times for his country, although it says much for his abilities that he captained the Springboks in each of those 29 Tests, losing just eight.

ABOVE Francois Pienaar in Pretoria, 1994

A distinguished sporting career in his teens led Pienaar to be at the forefront of a powerful Transvaal side in the early 1990s, when he earned his reputation.

In 1993 a Transvaal side with Pienaar as the captain won the inaugural Super 10 competition (a forerunner to the Super 12). They also picked up consecutive Currie Cup titles in 1993 and 1994.

During this time Pienaar forged a formidable partnership with Kitch Christie, the man who was to coach the Springboks at the 1995 World Cup. So Pienaar became the one and only choice as captain for that tournament.

The appointment of Andre Markgraaf as Springbok coach after the 1995 World Cup led to Pienaar's departure from South Africa and a famous sojourn in England.

Markgraaf had told Pienaar he would not figure in his plans and as the coach had been appointed, at the time, until the end of the 1999 World Cup it was clear that Pienaar needed to search for pastures new.

"I took the news on the chin, but I was hurt, I felt so bad, so miserable," he admitted.

"Adding insult to injury the coach had not even telephoned me with the news."

Predictably that announcement was greeted with astonishment across South Africa. Radio phone-ins and TV debates were packed with people who could not believe Pienaar had been axed.

Many believed Pienaar had been dropped as he was "too strong" for coach Markgraaf but whatever the rea-

sons it was clear his days in South Africa were numbered.

Markgraaf's decision was hardly borne out by results and a year later the Springboks went down to the British and Irish Lions, without Pienaar.

Pienaar was still keen to win his place back but the crucial intervention came from his World Cup coach, Kitch Christie. He told Pienaar to seriously consider the offer from English club Saracens, suggesting he would relish a new challenge.

In taking on that new challenge, Pienaar was lucky in that leaving South Africa he was able to join Nigel Wray's Saracens, a club steeped in history and owned by a man who loved the spirit of rugby.

A multi-millionaire, Wray is full of humility and even waited at Heathrow Airport for two hours to collect Pienaar and his wife, Nerine, on their arrival in England.

Pienaar finished off his playing career with Saracens, later becoming Chief Executive of Watford-based Premiership club, delivering the Tetley's Bitter Cup for them in 1998 before leaving in 2002, his footprints indelibly left in rugby's history.

OPPOSITE Francois Pienaar on the ball against Wasps in the 1998 Tetley Bitter Cup final (left) and holding the trophy aloft (above)

Quinnells

THE NAME QUINNELL HAS BEEN toasted and revered throughout the game, most notably in the clubhouses and alehouses of west Wales, for nigh on 35 years as one of the most famous dynasties in the rugby world.

The sweat and commitment of a life of toil at rugby's coalface has been shared across these decades by father Derek and sons Scott and Craig. And there is little likelihood that the pedigree of this most aristocratic of rugby bloodlines will diminish over the next few years with youngest scion Gavin already capped at under-21 level.

Throw in the fact that the wondrous fly-half Barry 'King' John, whose peerless talents flickered all too briefly on the international stage, is Derek's brother-in-law and the three lads' uncle and the Principality can claim with some justification to have an alternative Royal Family.

TOP RIGHT Father of the dynasty – Derek Quinnell – on the ball with the 1974 Lions

BELOW Derek Quinnell waits for a Welsh ball in 1980

To pick up the story from its early days, a raw-boned, red-haired back-row forward from Stradey Park, barely 22, was a surprise selection for the British and Irish Lions tour of New Zealand in 1971.

Carwyn James, the party's inspirational coach, saw something in the young man from Llanelli which had eluded the Welsh selectors up to that point. And the heroic greenhorn played a pivotal role, persistently collaring the dangerous All Blacks' scrum-half Sid Going in what turned out to be a triumphant and historic tour.

A Lion he may have been, but Derek remained uncapped by Wales until the dying moments of the following year's Five Nations' Championship. Finally, the great No 8 Mervyn Davies had to leave

the field due to injury late in the game against France at Cardiff. Desperate to get on to the (Arms) Park, young Derek muscled his way past battalions of Welsh constabulary, as well as the touch judge, to reach his promised land just before the referee blew for time.

Derek went on to win 23 caps with Wales and take part in two further Lions tours - to South Africa in 1974 and New Zealand again three years later. However, he is likely to be best remembered for his mighty contribution to two matches which have never been accorded international status but will live forever in rugby's collective consciousness.

Llanelli's 9-3 victory over the 1972-73 All Blacks owed much to Derek's commitment to the cause and knowledge of his opponents. Arguably, this is still the Scarlets' finest hour in front of their saucepan-worshipping fans.

A few weeks later, against the same opponents, he produced an equally telling performance for the Barbarians in a 23-11 victory regarded by many pundits as perhaps the greatest match ever played.

After his Llanelli team-mate Phil Bennett had sold not one but two dummies in front of his own posts early in proceedings, a staggering passage of play unfolded. At a crucial moment, Quinnell brilliantly took a pass at ankle height and off-loaded with aplomb. Seconds later, with Cliff Morgan drooling so lyrically in his BBC commentary, Gareth Edwards sprinted 10 yards to set the seal on a truly immortal try-scoring move.

Fast forward to the early 1990s, and the name Quinnell once again featured in the back rows of both Llanelli and Wales.

Eldest son Scott, now approaching the twilight of his career, made his international debut at No 8 against Canada late in 1993 and went on to score the try of the 1994 Five Nations' tournament as Wales clinched the title with a 24-15 victory over France in Cardiff.

The young buffalo at the base of the Welsh scrum was absolutely rampant that day and immediately found himself being compared with his father.

The arguments still rage as to whether Derek or Scott was the better player, but there is no doubt that at his peak Scott was a world-class No 8 whose bulldozing style gained the hard yards that were so valuable for every team in which he played. In retrospect, it is no surprise that these talents soon attracted offers from rugby league.

After his triumphant 1993-94 season, Scott, with a wife and baby to support, had little choice but to turn his back on a game that was still amateur and opt for the financial security of a £500,000 transfer to Wigan.

Scott's absence from rugby union lasted two years, but once professionalism had dawned in the wake of the 1995 World Cup he was back plying his trade with Richmond, a traditional London club awash with new money which eventually led it to ruin.

He won his 10th cap for Wales against the United States in January 1997 and went to South Africa with the Lions the following summer only for a groin injury to end his tour before the start of the Test series.

The injury niggled for another year before eventually clearing up. But it was a move back to Llanelli during the early part of the 1998-99 season which provided the impetus Scott's career had lacked at Richmond.

He was back to his best during the 1999 Five Nations and World Cup campaigns. He had the unenviable distinction of being the first player to be sin-binned in a Test against France but a year later captained Wales to their only victory over the Springboks.

Another Lions tour, to Australia, beckoned in 2001 and this time Scott played all three Tests - a series that the visitors were a trifle unlucky to lose 2-1. Then, at the end of the following season, he announced his retirement from the Welsh team after 52 caps and 11 tries, citing the increasing physical difficulty he encountered in giving his all for both club and country.

Many observers felt he was disillusioned by how easily Wales had unravelled during the 2002 Six Nations and preferred to concentrate on helping Llanelli to conquer Europe after a succession of near misses in the Heineken Cup.

Two seasons later, club rugby's blue-riband trophy still eluded the Scarlets, but a successful 2005 could yet see Scott bring down the curtain on an illustrious career with a final Lions tour to New Zealand. He insists he is not available for Sir Clive Woodward's squad, but don't bet against his inclusion.

Brother Craig, who is 29, looked likely to have a similar impact to Scott when he made his debut against Fiji in 1995, aged only 20. But it took another

three years, by which time he too had moved from Llanelli to Richmond, before he became established in Wales's second row.

When Richmond merged with London Irish and London Scottish in May 1999, Craig moved back to Wales, but instead of rejoining Llanelli, as Scott had, he went to Cardiff where he still plays. He won the last of his 32 caps in 2002 and it seems that his sheer size (he is 6ft 6in and weighs more than 20 stone) counts against him in a game which is dominated nowadays by fitness and mobility.

Now it seems as though the baton is about to pass to 20-year-old Gavin, a No 8 like Derek and Scott. Indeed, the 2004-05 season is bound to see both Scott and Gavin turning out together for Llanelli.

And given the inconsistency of Wales's pack at a time when their backs are among the most exciting in the game, it will surely not be long before the name of Quinnell appears again on an international team sheet.

ABOVE Gavin Quinnell playing for Llanelli against Newport, October 2003

OPPOSITE Craig Quinnell playing for Cardiff against Biarritz in 2004

Record Breakers

1. MOST TESTS AS A CAPTAIN
Will Carling (England) - 59

Will Carling led England through the most successful period in their history, winning Grand Slams in 1991, 1992 and 1995 and taking them to a World Cup Final in 1991.

Born in Bradford-on-Avon, Carling was handed the captaincy in the same year, 1988, as he made his England debut, aged just 22.

Undoubtedly Carling was lucky to preside over an exceptionally gifted group of players but he still captained the side a record 59 times and his role in England's heyday should not be underestimated.

Current Newcastle coach Rob Andrew was Carling's outside half in the glory days.

"Will bore the responsibility of being captain superbly," said Andrew. "As a centre he had great pace and power, qualities which were the perfect foil to Jeremy Guscott.

"It's difficult to find a weakness in his game."

The career of the Harlequins centre was not without controversy as he was sacked from the England captaincy when he called the RFU committee "57 old farts" in an off the cuff remark at the end of an interview in May 1995.

But after uproar and the refusal of any other England player to take on the captaincy Carling was reinstated in an embarrassing U-turn for the RFU.

He failed to make the step-up to a

TOP RIGHT Will Carling runs through the heart of the Welsh defence during England's 1995 Grand Slam campaign

Lions career, dropping out with injury after being selected for the 1989 tour and failing to win a Test match spot four years later.

Carling made the last of 72 Test appearances in 1997.

2. MOST TEST MATCH TRIES
David Campese (Australia) – 64

Before, during and after David Campese's 15-year international career he managed to pick up a few enemies along the way with his outspoken views. It must irk those enemies and fans of every nation, apart from Australia, that the wing from Randwick had the ability to walk the walk as well as talk the talk.

An on-field entertainer Campese certainly knew the way to the try line, crossing it 64 times in his 101 Tests, a remarkable strike rate in such a long career.

Campo, as he was universally known, perfected the goose-step. Not to be confused with the sidestep, Campese's trick was his change of pace and for more than a decade it left international opponents trailing in the dirt.

A World Cup winner in 1991 many people believe that it was the way Campese taunted England that made them change from their tried and tested forward game plan to one of an expansive nature in the final.

He was voted the Player of the Tournament at the 1991 World Cup and if he didn't score in the final he certainly left his mark on the semi-final win over New Zealand

Always with one eye on the unconsidered option, Campese didn't always get it right as Greg Martin will testify. The Wallaby wing threw Martin a risky pass near his own try line against the 1989 Lions. The ball went loose, Ieuan Evans pounced and the series went to the British and Irish visitors.

Campese made his debut against New Zealand in 1982, immediately opening

ABOVE David Campese leaves the field after his final match for Australia against the Barbarians 1996.

OPPOSITE David Campese running in a try for the Australian touring team of 1984

his account with a sensational try and by the time he arrived in Europe with the 1984 Grand Slam side his place as a rugby legend was guaranteed.

After he retired Campese managed the Australian Sevens squad to a bronze medal at the 1998 Commonwealth Games and in January 2002 was awarded his Order of Australia Medal (AM) for services to Rugby Union.

3. MOST CAPPED SCRUM-HALF
George Gregan (Australia) - 95

When Nick Farr-Jones retired from the Australia No 9 shirt it was always going to take a big player to fill those big shoes.

But in ACT Brumbies scrum-half George Gregan Australia found not only a superb replacement but a man who went on to win more Test caps than any No 9 before him.

Gregan was the lynchpin of one of the most successful international teams of the nineties, winning the World Cup (1999) and Tri Nations titles before being instrumental in Australia's series win against the Lions, in 2001.

Only the presence of the unforgettable John Eales as Australian captain prevented Gregan from getting his hands on the Wallaby armband until Eales' retirement in 2001, although he was vice captain for the four years before.

Born in Zambia Gregan made his debut in 1994 against Italy and became one of the most accomplished players, in any position, of his generation.

He initially made his name on the Sevens circuit and was also an accomplished cricketer.

Gregan was responsible for one of the most famous tackles in the history of the game, knocking the ball out of the hands of All Blacks wing Jeff Wilson as he was about to score a try to win the Bledisloe Cup in 1994.

BELOW George Gregan spins the ball out during the 1999 RWC semi-final against South Africa

Like Gareth Edwards in the 1970s Gregan is a devastating attacking threat, as well as being a great passer of the ball. In defence he has the ability to stop anyone.

4. MOST CONSECUTIVE TESTS
Sean Fitzpatrick (New Zealand) - 63

One of the greatest players to pull on an All Blacks jersey, once Sean Fitzpatrick made his Test debut in 1986 there was hardly any shifting him from the team.

The son of All Black centre Brian, Sean got his chance in the Test arena after the rebel Cavaliers tour to South Africa. Following that game the New Zealand rugby union picked a side, in 1986, dubbed The Baby Blacks of which Sean was a key component.

Fitzy's career saw him win 92 caps, while his run of 63 consecutive games saw him stay in the New Zealand team for a remarkable eight years. He enjoyed series wins against all the major nations and a World Cup Final win in 1987. Fitzy also captained his country a record 51 times.

The run that allows him to take his place in our list of record breakers would have gone on but the Auckland hooker was rested for an easy game, against Japan, in the 1995 World Cup pool stage.

As strong a scrummager as most props Fitzy was a massive presence around the field and in the line out for the All Blacks. He was the world's most-capped forward until Jason Leonard took his record. But by the end of the 2003 World Cup no other hooker had played more Tests.

A knee injury eventually ended his international career in 1997 and the All Blacks have struggled to replace him ever since.

In the New Zealand Rugby Greats book former New Zealand coach Laurie Mains said of him: "Following the tour of Australia and South Africa in 1992 it was obvious he was something special.

"He possessed the almost indefinable X-factor of which great All Black captains are made."

ABOVE Sean Fitzpatrick on line-out duty

Six Nations

THE MOST FAMOUS AND OLDEST rugby tournament in the world, the Six Nations Championship is revered throughout the rugby world. As England showed in 2004 a Six Nations Grand Slam is as hard to win as a Rugby World Cup.

England arrived at the 2004 RBS Six Nations Championship as reigning world champions. They not only failed to win the Grand Slam (victory in every one of their five matches) but also lost two games along the way to finish third.

France, who England beat in the 2003 Rugby World Cup semi-final, turned that form around to lift the 2004 Grand Slam. With Ireland winning at Twickenham it consigned England to their worst Championship for a decade.

This championship, now contested by England, France, Ireland, Scotland, Wales and Italy, embodies everything great about the game of rugby union and ensures hundreds of thousands of people pack into European stadiums every spring.

Rugby's first international, between England and Scotland was staged in 1871. Although those two sides plus Ireland and Wales played each other regularly the Championship didn't get it's moniker of the Five Nations until 1910, when the French were invited into the annual rugby festival.

France's first game was a trip to Swansea to take on Wales, a difficult

After staging rugby's first international in 1871, Scotland spent much of the intervening period as the bridesmaids of European rugby. In the 1920s that changed as they lifted their first Grand Slam.

More than 70,000 people crowded into Murrayfield in 1925 to see Scotland win 14-11.

France were in their 18th Championship before they claimed their first victory over England, in 1927, and it came by the slim margin of 3-0.

That French success was followed by a period of isolation. Amid allegations of professionalism in the French Leagues the national side was excluded from the Championship in the 1930s and they didn't return to the tournament until after the Second World War, in 1946.

In the last Championship before the War, Wales, Ireland and England shared the title; all three sides lost one match.

Despite having some great teams in the last century, the Irish side have only managed to deliver one Grand Slam, in 1948. Some 32,000 people packed

OPPOSITE Brilliant French scrum-half Dimitri Yachvili scores against England to secure the 2004 Grand Slam for France

BELOW Scotland vs Wales from 1927, the year Scotland and Ireland tied the Five Nations

start considering Wales' domination in the decade before. But the French managed, at least, to get on the scoreboard, although they did lose 49-14.

The French haven't conceded so many points in a Championship game since and their 37-0 defeat against England a year later, in 1911, remained in 2004 their biggest loss.

The years before the war essentially belonged to England as they only lost three games in the three years before 1914, taking three titles between 1910 and 1914.

ABOVE Welsh captain John Dawes chaired off the pitch after Wales' 1971 Grand Slam winning victory in France

into Ravenhill to see Ireland clinch their first Grand Slam with a 6-3 victory over Wales. Outside half Jackie Kyle and hooker Karl Mullen were at the centre of so much of the brilliant Irish play and the side scored ten tries in their four games, more than they'd achieved for 20 years.

The Welsh were also moving into a dominant period in their history, winning Grand Slams in 1950 and 1952 while only being out of the first two in the Championship once in the 1950s. England also enjoyed success later in the decade, taking their own Grand Slam in 1957.

In the 1960s Wales and France dominated the Championship, with seven outright wins between them.

France's greatest day arrived in 1968. A year after winning the Championship again they finally completed their first Grand Slam.

When you mention the 1970s one vision comes into the minds of rugby fans everywhere – Wales.

From 1969 to 1979, Wales came to power in the Five Nations and this time will be remembered as the golden era of Welsh rugby.

Winning the Triple Crown six times, the Welsh side were almost unstoppable. Only an outstanding French side prevented them from adding to the three Grand Slams achieved in this decade, with their own in 1977.

In 1976 Wales were at their best. Their lowest score in 1976 was 19 points and no side scored more than 13 points against them. Their total of 102 points was a Championship record.

One of the most endearing pictures in rugby's history shows one William (or Bill to everyone in the rugby world) Beaumont being chaired off the pitch, at Murrayfield, after England had clinched their first Grand Slam for 23 years, in 1980.

The four victories were built on the incredible England pack that not only delivered the Grand Slam but a prized and rare victory in the Parc des Princes (17-13), their first in Paris for 16 years. The success was, however, isolated for England and it was France who took over the decade, winning the title outright three times. The French feat included two Grand Slams and they even shared the title three more times.

It was left to Scotland to put down the real challenge to the French and in 1984 came their first Grand Slam for 46 years.

The final game in 1984 was the Grand Slam decider with both Scotland and France still unbeaten. Scotland triumphed 21-12 after falling 9-3 behind but being allowed back into the match by French indiscipline.

Ireland won the Triple Crown and the Championship, in 1985, with a 13-10 Dublin win over England, and it was Tom Kiernan who proved the hero dropping a vital, injury time, goal.

As Wales did in the 1970s so England started the 1990s winning the Grand Slam three times. They marked their dominance by taking the Triple Crown six times in eight seasons. They did it under one captain, Will Carling.

The 1991 Grand Slam was achieved after they won a two-way battle with the French, the crucial victory coming at Twickenham, 21-19. In 1992 they flew through the other four nations, scoring a Championship record 118 points (35 more than in 1991), only conceding 29 on their way to the Slam, scoring 15 tries.

The following year - 1993 - brought only two wins for Carling and they had to wait until 1995 for their final Grand

ABOVE Another iconic rugby photograph sees Bill Beaumont chaired off the Murrayfield pitch after England's victory secured the 1980 Grand Slam

Slam of the decade, and until Martin Johnson's side won it the next time, in 2003.

England may have dominated the middle period of the decade but they didn't get the start they needed. Scotland won the Grand Slam in 1990, again with a winner takes all showdown, with England on the final day of the Championship.

Scotland also ended the decade on top, clinching the 1999 Five Nations with a last weekend victory over the French, in Paris.

Wales had limped through the 1980s but worse was to come in 1990 when they suffered their first whitewash in the Five Nations.

Under the captaincy of Ieuan Evans they did buck the trend once, in 1994,

when they were Five Nations champions, losing one game, but winning it on a superior points difference.

Wales may have had little to cheer in the 1990s but they ended the decade on a high. With Cardiff Arms Park being redeveloped, Wales had decamped to Wembley for their home games. It was Clive Woodward's England, captained by Lawrence Dallaglio who arrived, hunting a Grand Slam.

With a Scott Gibbs try in the dying seconds, Wales delivered a sensational 32-31 victory.

Points difference was introduced to separate the teams in 1993, although it wasn't needed to decide the winner in that year, France taking the title with three wins.

France had to wait until the end of the decade to assert their supremacy on the Five Nations, taking back-to-back Grand Slams in 1997 and 1998.

In 1997 the records tumbled as the sides scored 53 tries and an incredible 511 points in ten matches. This smashed the previous best of 363, six years before.

France repeated the Grand Slam in 1998, in a Championship which saw Sunday play for the first time and a year later Lloyds-TSB paid £12 million for the privilege of sponsoring the title for the next two seasons.

Five became six in 2000, when Italy offered the Five Nations committee a proven club championship, good competition for their national sides and a venue, in Rome, that their supporters were dying to get to.

Although it took Italy until 2000 to kick off the Six Nations they did it in dramatic style, beating Scotland 34-20

They couldn't follow-up that win and the Italians lost 14 consecutive games.

However, their fortunes took an upward turn in 2003 with their best Championship performance, beating Wales and scoring a very respectable 100 points in their five games.

Clive Woodward's England ended four years of near misses by finally winning a Grand Slam in 2003. Between 1999 and 2002 England had a shocking

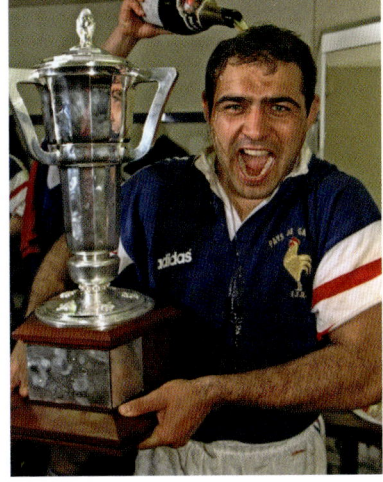

record in the last game of the Championship. In three of those four years they won all their games before falling at the final hurdle.

In 1999 it was Wales, 2000 Scotland and 2001 Ireland who beat them in the final match, although in 2002 France showed their abilities with a Grand Slam.

Those bad memories for the English team were banished to the history books in 2003. In this year Ireland and England arrived at the last game - again in Dublin - both unbeaten in a winner takes all Grand Slam showdown.

It was the first time, since 1995, that the Grand Slam (when England beat Scotland) could have been won by either team playing in the last match. Once again England held their nerve, this

time to triumph 42-6, Will Greenwood scoring two tries.

A year later they came into the Championship as hot favourites having just won the World Cup but the form-book went out of the window.

Ireland became the first side to win at Twickenham in the championship since 1997 and when England lost the last game of the Championship, 24-21, in Paris, France owned the Grand Slam. England were left a poor third.

Celebrations went on in Dublin as Ireland picked up their first Triple Crown (wins over the other home nations, England, Wales and Scotland) since 1985.

LEFT Raphael Ibanez, captain of the French team, celebrates their 1998 Grand Slam

BELOW Gordon D'Arcy (left) and Brian O'Driscoll (right) of Ireland celebrate winning the Triple Crown

Tri-Nations

WITH THE DAWN OF PROFESSIONAL rugby in 1995 it was inevitable that the game would engineer more high class and regular competition between nations and leading clubs.

The Northern Hemisphere had established their Five Nations in 1910 and although those in the south had survived on a diet of tours and the World Cup, it was only a matter of time before an annual competition was established.

There were fears that this regular competition would become stale but the Tri-Nations tournament, between Australia, South African and New Zealand, has been a huge success, each July and August.

Inevitably the new tournament - which kicked off in 1996 - has produced some great matches and when Rugby World magazine declared its best match of the period between 1990 and 2002 it was New Zealand's win over Australia at the opening of Stadium Australia, in 2000. In a ding-dong battle the All Blacks eventually snatched it 39-35.

With such long distances to travel - unlike in the Six Nations - the draw is all-important. New Zealand and Australia play their games in South Africa back-to-back and if the Springboks can get those games at the start of the tournament it increases their chances of getting off to a flying start.

1998 (their only Grand Slam), including a 29-15 victory in the last match against Australia.

In 1999 with the Rugby World Cup just around the corner normal Tri-Nations service was resumed with New Zealand topping the table. They made it despite a last weekend defeat to Australia, 28-7, in front of an astonishing 107,052 fans at Stadium Australia. The Wallabies would have taken the title with that win were it not for their thrilling 10-9 defeat in South Africa.

With the World Cup safely tucked up in the offices of the Australian Rugby Union it was probably fitting that they followed up this success by winning their first Tri-Nations trophy, in 2000.

To win the World Cup is the ultimate sign of success. To follow it up ten months later with the Tri-Nations ensured that this Australian team would be ranked among the best the world has ever seen. Captain John Eales said: "The great thing is there's so much depth in Australian rugby, a lot more than we had

From the outset the Tri-Nations broke new ground with bonus points for tries scored. Although you didn't need recourse to a calculator to see who'd won it in the first year (1996) as New Zealand were victorious in all four of their matches. Australia in particular were beaten 43-6 in that year.

The All Blacks made it two titles out of two, in 1997, but they fell a long way short of the hat trick. The new, exciting South African team won every game in

OPPOSITE Jonah Lomu evades the tackle of Stephen Larkham during their Bledisloe Cup match at Stadium Australia, 2000. New Zealand won the epic match 39-35

BELOW Christian Cullen of New Zealand is tackled by Andre Venter of South Africa during their 1997 Tri-Nations match at Ellis Park in Johannesburg

a few years ago. The Tri-Nations showed that the new generation is just around the corner and coming through fast."

In 2001 Australia completed an incredible double, beating the British and Irish Lions 2-1 in their Test series and then going on to retain the Tri-Nations in an incredible few months of rugby for the Wallabies.

This time, in 2001, they needed a late, late try from Toutai Kefu to get a 29-26 win over New Zealand and they lifted the trophy, before their captain John Eales, retired.

For the second successive year Australia overcame defeat in their first game, this time 20-15 to South Africa, to win the Tri-Nations.

As if to stress how hard it is to take the upper hand in the southern hemisphere a monumental New Zealand effort in 2002 prevented the Australians from completing the hat trick. Again the champions failed to win every game, the All Blacks suffering a 16-14 reversal in Australia. New Zealand did beat them 12-6 when the sides met for the first game of the tournament.

The Springboks struggled in the initial years of the Tri-Nations and in 2002 they finished bottom again, this time with one win, 33-31 against Australia.

The last Tri-Nations tournament before the 2003 World Cup should have provided a great form line for rugby's ultimate competition. However, it ended with a victory for New Zealand over Australia, a triumph that the All Blacks failed to repeat in the World Cup semi-finals.

The Kiwis came into that last game, in 2003, against Australia with the tournament already won after a 19-11 victory over South Africa, who finished bottom of the table again. It was the All Blacks' third Grand Slam.

If the Tri-Nations satisfied the need for great international competition the Super 12 bridged the gap between domestic competition and Test matches.

When professionalism arrived in rugby union in 1995 the southern hemisphere was far quicker out of the starting blocks than their counterparts in the north. Crucial to this strategy was a top class tournament that fed the national teams. The progress of the current Super 12 started in the mid-1980s with the South Pacific Championships or Super 6. This early tournament even involved Fiji but the Super 12 is now restricted to

the best provinces from Australia, New Zealand and South Africa.

After a break forced on the organisers by the withdrawal of New South Wales, the competition was relaunched as a Super 10, in 1993, comprising of four sides from New Zealand, three from South Africa, two from Australia and one from the Pacific Islands, which this time was Western Samoa.

That 1993 final - after the sides were split into two pools - was won by Transvaal (South Africa) who beat Auckland 20-17.

ABOVE Corne Krige, the South Africa captain, looks dejected as his team loses at home by a record margin of 52-16 against New Zealand 2003

The offical declaration of professional rugby allowed the tournament to take its current shape and it was renamed Super 12.

The omission of a Pacific Island team - and the increase to 12 sides - allowed the big three an additional side each in the new revamped tournament. This decision was significant for the Pacific Islanders as their exclusion hampered their development.

The clamour for an Islands team to be reinstated into a new Super 14 was deafening at the 2003 Rugby World Cup.

OPPOSITE The Crusaders celebrate their 31-13 victory over the Brumbies in the 2002 Super 12 final

BELOW Keven Mealamu of the Blues charges past Richard McCaw of the Crusaders during the Blues' 21-17 victory in the 2003 Super 12 final

Auckland were the first Super 12 winners, with the tournament in a one pool league, beating Natal 45-21 in the final.

From its inception it has become a pioneering tournament. They were the first to offer a bonus for tries scored and started a scoring system that was later adopted in England by the Zurich Premiership.

In 2002 the Crusaders (Canterbury - New Zealand) became the first side to win the tournament undefeated in any of the matches on their way to the final, where they beat the 2001 winners the ACT Brumbies (Australia), 31-13.

In 2003 New Zealand's victory in the Tri-Nations was proceeded by a Super 12 victory for the Auckland Blues, 21-17, over their neighbours from Canterbury.

Upsets

UPSETS ABOUND IN THE WORLD OF sport, that's what makes it great. Here are some of the most amazing from the world of international rugby...

AUSTRALIA 11 TONGA 16
Brisbane 1973

Many things are credited for Australia's rise in the rugby world. One of the most significant milestones in their recent history was their lowest point when Tonga humiliated them in 1973.

No one Down Under saw the defeat coming as the Tongans had limped through their Australia tour losing to New South Wales and the ACT. They arrived on the Sunshine Coast for a Test match few expected them to win. They had already lost the first Test 30-12 in Sydney.

Win they did though - in front of 9,563 fans at Ballymore – and they scored a staggering four tries to inflict the worst defeat in Australia's history. Australia even led, 11-8, going into the last ten minutes.

The Australian rugby union, as we learn from the book Wallaby Gold never forgot the lessons from the defeat.

Peter Loane, from that team said: "It was also the start of something. We started looking seriously at things like the scrum and line out.

"We always had brilliant backs but securing possession was the problem.

"But something had been started and 11 years after losing to Tonga, Australia won the Grand Slam (in Great Britain) and of course the World Cup in 1991 was the zenith."

NEW ZEALAND 10 ENGLAND 16
Auckland 1973

Victories in New Zealand are rare enough. For a side who had just lost to Ireland and Wales and only beaten Fiji by a point it was surely a dream too far.

England's hopes were also dampened by three defeats in provincial matches in New Zealand.

The 1973 England side clearly hadn't read the script as John Pullin's side pulled off England's first victory in New Zealand for 37 years.

England scored three tries, through a sensational forward-powered performance, the decisive one coming from Tony Neary.

This great result wasn't even planned as the side was due to tour Argentina until the trip was called off under the threat of terrorist attack.

The book Men in Black saw England's achievement in the context of the All Blacks performance.

"While not wishing to detract from the merit of England's win we feel this must have been one of the most inept displays ever by an All Black team."

SOUTH AFRICA 12
SOUTH AMERICAN JAGUARS 21
Bloemfontein 1982

This was another example of the underdogs getting hammered in the first Test only to roar back in the second to beat their more illustrious opponents.

The Springboks had posted 50 points on the Jaguars in the first Test but in the return match they had planned without the genius of Hugo Porta.

The Jaguars were a team made up predominantly of Argentineans but they decided to forget about trying to win the battle up front in the second Test.

Porta, who many consider the greatest outside half in the history of the game, took centre stage. It was one of the greatest one-man displays in rugby's history, as he scored all 21 points for the Jaguars. It was the record points total by one player against the Springboks.

With the South Africans banned from international rugby due to Apartheid it didn't rank as an official Test match but the South Africans and the South Americans regarded it as nothing less.

The Springboks made no changes to their team despite the initial 50-point hammering.

"The Springbok defeat in an often ill-tempered match is arguably the biggest upset in South African rugby history," explained Chris Greyvenstein in Springbok Rugby - an Illustrated History.

"Behind a vastly improved pack, Porta proved that, at 31, he was still a

BELOW Legendary Argentinian number 10, Hugo Porta was instrumental in the South American Jaguars extraordinary defeat of South Africa

masterful fly half and he guided his band of no-hopers to a thoroughly deserved victory."

NAMIBIA 26 IRELAND 15
Windhoek 1991

You can take your pick from this shocking tour by the Irish, when they lost both games against Namibia. Although the second game was fractionally worse because at least for this Test they couldn't say they were taken by surprise.

The altitude of Namibia did contribute to the first Test defeat, 15-6.

This was no second string outfit either as ten of the team that had played at Twickenham in the Five Nations were in the side and Ireland led 12-10 at half time.

Great Irish players like Nick Popplewell, Neil Francis (who went off in the second half with concussion), Donal Lenihan, Rob Saunders, Brendan Mullin and Jim Staples were in the side. Although they were without captain Phil Matthews because of a stomach upset.

But in Namibia they found a committed and passionate opposition that harried them from the start, and ran in five tries, against two from Staples and Vince Cunningham for Ireland.

WALES 13 WESTERN SAMOA 16
Cardiff 1991

Wales finished third in the 1987 World Cup and with the pool stages in 1991 based in the Principality they were cast as one of the favourites to make the knockout stages.

They knew little about the men from the tiny island of Western Samoa but this incredible victory provided a platform to launch the careers of some of the island's great rugby stars.

When you consider the side that day included players like Mat Keenan, Apollo Perelini, Pat Lam, Steve Bachop, Brian Lima, Frank Bunce, and Peter Fatialofa the captain it is perhaps a wonder how Wales got so close.

In many ways the victory did European rugby a big favour as we got to see those players in our leagues and they inspired a new generation of Samoans into the game.

ABOVE The Welsh look singularly unimpressed by the Samoan Haka prior to their shock defeat

"It's the greatest day in our lives. It's a great day in our rugby history," Fatialofa said.

Manager Tate Simi added: "To beat Wales at the Arms Park has always been a moment to cherish and this is very much so for the Western Samoan players."

IRELAND 17 ENGLAND 3
Dublin 1993

England fully expected to extend their six-year unbeaten run in Dublin when they arrived in 1993, only to be on the end of a shocking defeat.

Ireland fly-half Eric Elwood was the main destroyer scoring 12 points, Mick Galwey grabbing the only try, in the 80th minute, against an England team that had won back-to-back Grand Slams in 1991 and 1992.

The Irish swarmed over the England pack, getting on top and then disrupting the back line.

The match signalled the end of an era for England with six of the side - Jon Webb, Stuart Barnes, Jeff Probyn, Wade Dooley, Mike Teague and Peter Winterbottom - never playing international rugby again!

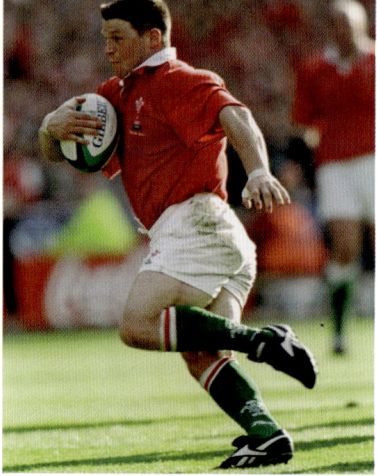

WALES 32 ENGLAND 31
Wembley 1999

England had watched France win back-to-back Grand Slams in 1997 and 1998 and it looked like it was going to be their turn in the last Five Nations of the decade.

Victories over Scotland, Ireland and France sent England to face Wales with the Grand Slam on offer.

Wales had endured an awful Championship on the back of an awful decade and had lost to both Scotland and Ireland.

Added to that the National Stadium in Cardiff was a building site, due to the building of the Millennium Stadium and the game was switched to Wembley Stadium, London.

The Principality emptied to fill Wembley and they had a certain kicker called Neil Jenkins who was always capable of keeping his side in the game.

England - captained by Lawrence Dallaglio - were huge favourites and had raced into a 25-18 lead and should have tied the game up by half time. If it wasn't for Jenkins' boot they would have done.

In the second half England were still coasting and their confidence was typified in their decision to kick for touch late on instead of taking the points on offer, from the boot of Jonny Wilkinson, with the score 31-25.

A Wales penalty followed and Jenkins suddenly had the visitors back in their own half with the match almost over.

A rehearsed move involving Scott Quinnell and Scott Gibbs suddenly put Gibbs in the clear dancing through the England defence and over the line.

Jenkins kicked the winning conversion and a nation celebrated!

SCOTLAND 19 ENGLAND 13
Murrayfield 2000

The bookmakers made England 1-12 to win this match at Murrayfield. For the second year running Clive Woodward's side arrived on the last day of the

ABOVE Andy Nicol secures the loose ball and an improbable victory for Scotland over England in 2000

Championship needing a win to clinch their first Grand Slam since 1995.

Woodward hadn't planned for an Edinburgh downpour and his side proved totally unable to cope with the rain or to change from one game plan to another.

It all started well, as it had done 12 months earlier against Wales, with a Lawrence Dallaglio try but they never put the Scots away and Duncan Hodge pounced with all 19 points.

England led 10-9 at the interval and after the match England coach Clive Woodward said: "It feels exactly like 1999 (when England lost to Wales). I can't say any more than that."

Scotland coach Ian McGeechan added: "My team had to play out of their skins and they did. They didn't let England settle."

VII (Sevens)

THE SHORTENED VERSION OF THE 15-a-side game has its roots in Scotland, inspired by a butcher from Melrose, Ned Haig.

In 1883 Haig was looking for a way to make money for the Melrose club and hit upon the idea of varying the game.

"Want of money made us rack our brains as to what was to be done to keep the club from going to the wall," Haig was later to recall.

"And the idea struck me that a football tournament might prove attractive.

"But as it was hopeless to think of having several games in one afternoon with fifteen players on each side, the teams were reduced to seven."

The Melrose Sevens – which still runs today – proved to be a sensational success, not only saving the Scottish border club but inspiring a new avenue for the game.

Almost 2,000 people packed into the Melrose ground in April 1883 to see the Sevens contested by a number of Borders clubs.

The ladies of Melrose presented the Melrose Cup to the host club and the name has forever been entwined with Sevens. Even today the Rugby World Cup Sevens trophy is called the Melrose Cup.

Other Borders clubs like Gala and Hawick were quick to run their own Sevens tournaments but it did take many decades to take hold in the rest of the rugby world. The first World Cup was staged more than 100 years later.

After the First World War a Sevens circuit grew up in the Scottish Borders and to this day most of them still thrive,

Sevens becoming a big part of the Scottish rugby culture.

Scotland – which staged that first World Cup in 1993 – has always remained the spiritual home of Sevens but closely challenging its place is Hong Kong.

Perhaps the most famous Sevens event in the world, the Hong Kong tournament has allowed some big stars, including Jonah Lomu and David Campese their first taste of international rugby.

Hong Kong's annual jamboree kicked off in 1976 and in the early years the title was confined to southern hemisphere sides although England has produced an incredible hat trick of wins from 2002-04.

The staging of the Five or Six Nations at the same time as the Hong Kong event had allowed the southern hemisphere their opportunity to dominate, until England started to prioritise Sevens as a feeder for the 15-a-side game.

Tokkie Smith was the Ned Haig of the 1970s driving the Hong Kong Sevens forward when he was greeted with some scepticism in the early days.

Today the Hong Kong Sevens is one of the 'must-do' events for rugby fans and players from all over the world.

The first Hong Kong Sevens, in 1976, attracted 12 teams and a one-day crowd of 3,000 but today the tournament stretches over three days and there are 40,000 fans (many of them in fancy dress) packed in on finals day.

"Basically there have been no excuses to miss the Hong Kong Sevens," explained John Blondin in his book Rugby World Cup Sevens – Divine Intervention.

"A survey among the spectators will reveal that for many they have been attending for years as it is in their blood."

Hong Kong was the scene of the second World Cup Sevens in 1997, where

OPPOSITE Jonah Lomu with the 2001 Melrose Cup, so named after the Melrose Club, the pioneers of the Sevens tournament

BELOW Pat Sanderson of England beats the tackle of Pablo Gomez Cora of Argentina as England win the 2004 Hong Kong World Sevens

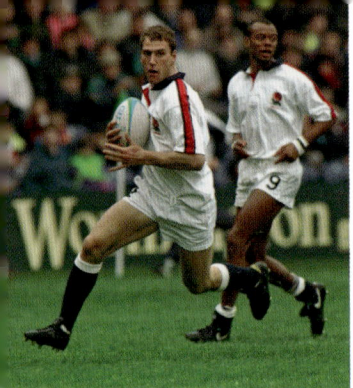

Fiji took the crown, but the first World Cup was held in Murrayfield, four years earlier.

In 1993 an unfancied England team were victorious. England's lack of Sevens pedigree made them outsiders but as their team included players like Lawrence Dallaglio, Matt Dawson and Andrew Harriman it is no wonder they did so well! England beat Australia in the final.

Qualifying tournaments were needed in 1997 such was the interest being generated across the world.

In 1997 there was a public holiday declared in Fiji when they lifted the World Cup, in Hong Kong, beating South Africa 24-21 in the final.

In 2001 New Zealand became the third different winner, taking the trophy with a 31-12 victory over Australia.

Former Australian Sevens captain Richard Graham explains the importance of the seven-a-side game in Gordon Bray's enthralling book, The Australian Rugby Companion.

Graham says: "Sevens is not, and never will be, a substitute for the 15-a-side game. Both have their own identity.

"However, the famous Hong Kong Sevens tournament can certainly take credit for revitalising many of the skills of the longer game."

In 1999 the IRB harnessed the lure of Sevens with an international event or World Series. This Series attempts to take the game, rather like Formula One does in motor racing, all round the world.

The World Series has introduced the game into many new territories. Since its inception the World Series has been played in 16 countries across five continents and no fewer than 46 countries have participated.

New Zealand dominated the World Series in its early years, winning the first four competitions in 2000, 2001, 2002 and 2003.

The Kiwis may have won the first four tournaments but England's rise has ensured they haven't had it all their own way.

In 2003 New Zealand only won the series – points were given at each of the seven tournaments – by four points, the result not decided until the final leg in London.

In England the magnificent Middlesex Sevens was one of the highest profile casualties of the professional era.

The Middlesex Sevens regularly attracted 60,000 people to Twickenham for an end of season party not bettered anywhere in Europe.

The English clubs demanded their own season finale and pushed the Middlesex Sevens into a start of the season slot that has failed to attract anywhere near the attention, crowds or standard of teams.

Rugby Sevens made its debut at the 1998 Commonwealth Games in Kuala Lumpur, where New Zealand won gold, repeating the feat in Manchester four years later. Fiji picked up the silver medal on both occasions.

At the 2002 Commonwealth Games in Manchester, the five sessions of Sevens attracted 130,000 spectators, second only

ABOVE Rupeni Caucaunibuca of Fiji breaks free to score a try during the Fiji v South Africa Men's Rugby Sevens semi-final at the 2002 Commonwealth Games

to the numbers watching the athletics.

The biggest Sevens event in the world is the Rosslyn Park Schools Tournament which annually attracts over 3,000 schoolchildren from all over the world.

In 2004 there was a team from Romania in the Rosslyn Park Schools Sevens, sponsored by the Wooden Spoon Society. And two years earlier a side from the Future Hope Foundation, in Calcutta, was represented.

Ivybridge Community College beat Millfield in the 2004 Open final, Wycombe High School taking the girls' title.

World Cup

AS RUGBY UNION MOVED FROM being an amateur to a professional game in the 1980s it was inevitable that a World championship would be established and in the summer of 1987 the Rugby World Cup was born. Since then a tournament has been held every four years.

RUGBY WORLD CUP 1987
Winners: **New Zealand**
Venue: **Australia and New Zealand**
Sixteen teams were invited to enter the first Rugby World Cup in 1987 as the game embarked on a new era that many feared would end with that first tournament. But from humble beginnings the tournament has grown and grown.

Throughout history the New Zealand All Blacks had proved themselves to be the most successful team in the rugby world so it was fitting that it was their captain, David Kirk, who lifted the trophy after his side dominated the tournament.

From the very first match, which New Zealand won 70-6 against Italy, no one came close to stopping the All Blacks relentless march to the title. Even in the final, against France they only conceded nine points!

Grant Fox was the New Zealand hero with 126 points and there was an unforgettable semi-final between France and Australia when Serge Blanco finished off a length of the field, injury time try as the Wallabies bowed out 30-24.

The home nations were sceptical about the concept but for Wales it represented their most successful World Cup to date as they finished third, beat-

ing England in the quarter-final, 16-3, and Australia in the third-fourth play-off, 22-21.

The games in Australia struggled to pull in the big crowds but in New Zealand, helped by the success of the hosts, things were different. The tournament brought 600,000 people through the turnstiles and a final profit of £1million.

RUGBY WORLD CUP 1991
Winners: **Australia**
Venue: **England, Scotland, Ireland, France and Wales**

With the success of 1987 behind them the International Rugby Board developed a far more ambitious tournament four years later, 40 countries starting a qualifying process that brought 16 teams to the Rugby World Cup finals.

The 1991 World Cup was significant for a number of reasons not least because it allowed Australia to emerge as a major force in the rugby world but

it also signalled the rise of the underdog. Western Samoa, as they were known then, changed everything we had believed about rugby's world order. They won a sensational 16-13 victory over Wales and only lost by nine points to eventual winners Australia.

The tournament opened in the magnificent setting of Twickenham, New Zealand winning the first match 18-12 against England. The reigning champion All Blacks failed to keep winning, though, bowing out in the semi-finals against Australia.

The Wallabies may have won the final, 12-6 against Will Carling's England, but they certainly didn't get things their own way. They needed an injury time try from Michael Lynagh to overcome Ireland at Lansdowne Road in the quarter-finals, 19-18.

But their ability to beat both New Zealand and England in the space of seven days made them worthy world champions, Australia scrum-half Nick Farr-Jones taking the Webb Ellis Cup from Her Majesty the Queen, after a final where prop Tony Daly scored the only try.

OPPOSITE David Kirk scores against France in the 1987 Cup final

BELOW John Eales and Tony Daley of Australia celebrate victory over England and a dejected Will Carling in the Rugby World Cup final of 1991

RUGBY WORLD CUP 1995
Winners: **South Africa**
Venue: **South Africa**

With Apartheid banished to the history books and the Springboks welcomed back into the rugby world there was only one place to hold the 1995 Rugby World Cup - South Africa.

This World Cup also benefited from being held in one country. When Nelson Mandela - the country's president - walked out on to Ellis Park to meet the teams for the final - New Zealand and South Africa - wearing a replica of South Africa captain Francois Pienaar's No 6 shirt the game had finally booked its place on the global stage.

Before the first match Mandela told the assembled players at the opening ceremony: "Your presence here affirms the unity in diversity, the humanity in healthy contest that our young democracy has come to symbolise. South Africa keenly appreciates your love and support. South Africa opens its arms and its heart to welcome you all."

The tournament was rugby's last as an amateur sport and it ended in sensational style, South Africa outside-half Joel Stransky kicking the winning drop goal in extra time to give his side a 15-12 victory over New Zealand.

England had come into the 1995 World Cup as one of the favourites. However, the Five Nations Grand Slam champions had to be content with fourth place after meeting a young All Blacks wing called Jonah Lomu in the semi-finals. The New Zealander trampled all over England's hopes with four amazing tries. Many people felt that England had played their "World Cup final" a week earlier when they beat Australia with a late drop goal from Rob Andrew, winning the quarter-final 25-22.

South Africa captain Francois Pienaar summed up the tide of pride and passion that had engulfed the Rainbow Nation during the tournament when, after the final victory, he said: "We did not have 63,000 fans behind us today, we had 43 million South Africans."

RUGBY WORLD CUP 1999

Winners: **Australia**
Venue: **England, Wales, Scotland, Ireland and France**

The 1999 Wallabies earned their place in rugby's history by becoming the first side to lift the Webb Ellis Cup twice when captain John Eales was handed the magnificent trophy from Her Majesty The Queen on 6 November at the Millennium Stadium.

The triumph not only represented their domination of the final, where they beat France 35-12, but their domination of the whole tournament. Where defence was supreme, they conceded just one try in the whole of their six-game campaign, and that to USA when they were giving a raft of their back-up players a chance to shine.

The final was in many ways an anticlimax to the France v New Zealand game, at Twickenham, which was without doubt one of the greatest games in rugby union history.

With the French battered by Jonah Lomu into a 14-point deficit they looked to be on their way out until they staged a sensational comeback to take the game 43-31, to make the final. It was French rugby at its best, full of flair and

with the focus of the attack coming from every position.

Lomu had once again been England's nadir scoring a try at Twickenham as the Kiwis won 30-16. That effectively knocked Martin Johnson's side out of the tournament. England's defeat ensured they finished second in their pool and were subjected to a midweek play-off before the South Africans inflicted the final blow in the quarter-finals.

For the first time none of the four Home Nations made the semi-finals, Ireland not even making the quarters and therefore having to suffer the ignominy of qualifying for the 2003 tournament.

ABOVE Tim Horan charges forward against France during the 1999 Rugby World Cup final

RUGBY WORLD CUP 2003
Winners: **England**
Venue: **Australia**

The Rugby World Cup had been the domain of the southern hemisphere nations before 2003 when Clive Woodward's England shook-up the rugby world with a victory that catapulted his players into super star status.

As it had done in 1995 victory came down to a drop goal. Only this time it arrived from the right boot of Jonny Wilkinson with just over one minute of extra time to go in a pulsating final between England and Australia.

The full 80 minutes and almost all of extra time had failed to split England and Australia and they stood locked at 17-17 before Wilkinson struck to send the Webb Ellis Cup to Twickenham.

The 2003 tournament was widely acknowledged as the best World Cup to date with more spectators, a bigger television audience and a larger profit for the International Board to re-invest in the game than ever before.

The hosts Australia made it into the final by beating the New Zealand All Blacks 22-10, while England had to overcome Wales in the quarter-finals and France in the semis, after both times going behind. Clive Woodward's side became kings of the comeback in this tournament, not only headed by Samoa in the pool stage but by Australia in the final.

South Africa failed to make the last four for the first time since their re-admission into international sport, New Zealand beating a weakened France side in the third-fourth play-off.

X-Codes

STUDENTS OF RUGBY LEAGUE WILL have taken great satisfaction in the fact that the two tries scored in the rugby union World Cup Final of 2003 were scored by former practitioners of the 13-man code.

Lote Tuquiri, the massive Fijian-born wing representing Australia, kicked off proceeding by beating his fellow convert, England's Jason Robinson, to a high ball to score first. But Robinson got his own back by touching down for the eventual winners. League followers would have taken little comfort from the way the flow of players from one code to another has been reversed in the last 10 years.

Tuquiri was one of three Australian backs hijacked from league who played in the final - Wendell Sailor and Mat Rogers were the others - while Robinson is perhaps the best player ever to negotiate the

cross from the traditional game of the north of England to the 15-man contest.

A true rugby superstar in any language, Robinson's introduction to the England squad in the 2001 Six Nations was greeted with incredulity by some of the more experienced members of the press pack who follow the red-rose brigade around the international circuit.

Fast-forward to the Lions tour of 2001 when Robinson captivated some of the more one-eyed union followers with his devastating opening try in the first Test at Brisbane's Gabba. From then on Robinson was 'one of us' and his impact in league's newly-paid brother has been immense.

Prior to 1995, it had virtually been one-way traffic. Union players struggling

ABOVE Former rugby leaguer Jason Robinson scores England's try in the 2003 Rugby World Cup Final

ABOVE David Watkins was a superstar at Salford

David Watkins, who steered Newport to victory over the All Blacks from fly-half in 1963, won 21 union caps for Wales and was a 1966 Lions tourist. League scouts had coveted him for a long time and he took the plunge in 1967 when he signed for Salford. Salford's normal gate was around 4,000 but 16,000 turned up to watch him drop two goals and score a try on his debut. He stayed in league until retiring in 1979 after one season with Swinton and clocked up more than 1,000 points, 16 Welsh league caps and six appearances for Great Britain to add to his union haul.

In retirement Watkins was the driving force behind the Cardiff Blue Dragons rugby league club and lured Steve Fenwick, Tom David, Paul Ringer and Brynmor Williams to the professional rank. But the experiment ended in 1984 as the Welsh public failed to warm to league. Watkins recently explained: "There was a 'them and us' situation between league and union and we had to bring a lot of players from the north of England. If people were seen training with the Blue Dragons and they didn't make it there was no way back for them into union."

to meet the demands of juggling sport with a full-time job and family life were more than willing to take the cash to go north and play league. It gave them financial security and more importantly they were treated like professional athletes in that they had rest periods away from the game and daytime training rather than trying to squeeze in shifts at the local bank, building site or casualty unit to make ends meet.

Welsh rugby union, in particular, suffered hugely in the 1920s when their most talented players went to league because of the financial difficulties at home and during the amateur days Wales saw some of its greatest players defect.

The fabled Welsh fly-half factory was pumping out sublimely gifted No 10s when Watkins jumped ship and Barry John seamlessly slipped into his boots. But when Jonathan Davies went north Wales lost their only truly world-class back.

In 1989, after a superb career with Neath, Llanelli and Wales, Davies, to the consternation of the Welsh public, joined Widnes. Anyone who thought the quicksilver fly-half would be found out in league was swiftly put right as Davies added bulk to his speed and won 13 Great Britain league caps. In 1994, by now a Warrington player, Davies scored one of the most memorable tries ever seen at Wembley as Great Britain beat Australia 8-4 and was named 'Man of Steel'. He remains the best union player ever to make a success of league. Strangely, few of England's leading players ever seemed to switch codes – the dynamic wing Keith Fielding was a notable exception - but in the days of

'shamateurism' there were ways and means of keeping them in union.

League's first real contribution to union, apart from a brief period in 1996 when players were loaned to the 15-man game, was on the 1997 Lions tour of South Africa. Players such as Scott Gibbs, John Bentley and Alan Tait had all played league and with professionalism in its infancy in union they showed the tour party the way. Martin Johnson's team were the first paid Lions and the input from the cross-coders was invaluable in securing victory over the Springboks.

TOP LEFT Jonathan Davies' move from Llanelli to Widnes was a disaster for Welsh rugby

BELOW Jonathan Davies' first game back for Wales, vs Australia in 1996

In money terms, the boot is on the other foot with rugby union having far deeper pockets nowadays and union coaches trawl league for the brightest talent. England coach Sir Clive Woodward was instrumental in Robinson's move to Sale and half of Henry Paul's first contract with Gloucester was paid by the RFU. Iestyn Harris's move south to Cardiff and Wales, the land of his father, reputedly cost £1.5 million and has taken a fair length of time to yield dividends.

Woodward even employs Phil Larder, the ex-rugby league coach, as his defensive expert, and Wigan legend Joe Lydon has been looking after the national sevens team in recent times. Lydon's former club and Great Britain team-mate, Shaun Edwards, is a coach at Wasps; indeed, most union sides have a league coach of some sort lurking in the background.

Rob Ackerman of Wales and four league clubs is enjoying success as the coach of Glasgow Hawks and France's Grand Slam of 2004 was based on a formidable defence marshalled by Englishman Dave Ellis, a former league player and coach.

Now that league is played in the summer, some players combine the codes. Liam Botham plays for both Leeds Tykes and Leeds Rhinos and the South African Japie Mulder was scheduled to do the same until injury intervened.

The fact that union is enjoying an upturn in popularity has led to various people sounding the death knell for league. It is true that the game has failed to take off in the south of England (and Jonny Wilkinson is unlikely to switch despite Larder's assertion that he would be a sensational league player) but the two codes have much to contribute to each other, as Woodward already knows.

OPPOSITE Henry Paul breaks through the Wasps defence in the 2003 Zurich Premiership Final

BELOW Rugby league hero Shaun Edwards is doing a fantastic job as coach of London Wasps

Young Ones

THERE ARE NOT VERY MANY records in rugby's history books that are out of the telescopic sights of Jonny Wilkinson, but even he will never be able to tick off the landmark of being England's youngest ever player on his bedroom wall-chart.

He got close though. His debut as a replacement against Ireland in 1998 came at the age of 18 years and 314 days and he was trumpeted as England's most fresh-faced representative for 71 years.

However, Wilkinson is not even the youngest fly-half to play for England as that honour goes to Colin Laird who pulled on the white No 10 jersey before running out against Wales on 15

ABOVE Jonny Wilkinson in action against Australia aged just 19. Australia won 76-0 but Jonny was to get his revenge

January 1927, aged 18 years and 134 days, to help his team to an 11-9 win.

Wilkinson even had to settle for a place down the list of England's youngest captains when he was picked to lead the side against Italy in the 2003 Six Nations at the age of 23. Go back a mere 15 years and you will find that Will Carling was appointed captain at the age of 22.

Carling, who was in the Army before leaving to concentrate on his business career, was deemed officer material on

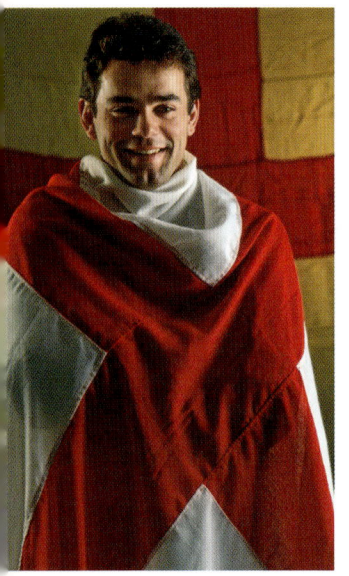

and off the park by England manager Geoff Cooke who made him skipper for the home test against the Wallabies in 1988.

Carling was the youngest England captain for 57 years and barely out of short trousers, but he inspired his side to win 28-19 although the new boss had to be helped from the field after being knocked senseless with moments left. It looked as if the job was his for the next decade but he eventually returned to the playing ranks in 1996.

The New Zealand No 8 Taine Randell was entrusted with the captaincy of the All Blacks at the tender age of 21. And plenty of other countries have given the captaincy to a young shaver from the ranks over the years. The legendary Welsh scrum-half Gareth Edwards was tossed the metaphorical armband aged 20 and was the youngest rugby player to be awarded an MBE seven years later before, yes you've guessed it, Wilkinson got his gong at 23.

A fresh-faced Ken Catchpole led Australia on his debut in 1961 against Fiji and gave his side the mother of all dressing downs at the break after a poor first half. The Wallabies went on to win 24-6.

It must be something to do with scrum-halves who have to be pretty vocal carrying out their normal duties, but the hugely talented Nigel Melville was also England captain on his debut against Australia in 1984. He had the misfortune to run into the Grand Slam team of Mark Ella and Co who took the game 19-3. Melville's playing career was eventually curtailed by injury and he now plies his trade as a grey-round-the-temples coach at Gloucester and general-purpose rugby guru.

When the All Blacks made Jonah Lomu their youngest player by handing him his debut against France in 1994 aged 19 years and 45 days they knew what they were doing. The French actually won that day, 22-8, but the young Lomu was to terrorise defences for the next nine years even though he has recently been handicapped by a debilitating kidney disease. The hulking winger is actually the oldest of the youngest players amongst the major rugby playing nations.

Winger Jack Hartley was 18 years and 18 days when he played for South Africa against Great Britain in 1891 whilst Claude Dourthe was 18 years and seven days when making his debut for France against Romania in 1966.

Scotland can lay claim to having the youngest international debutant in the shape of Ninian Finlay who was 17 years and 36 days old when running out against England in 1875. His countryman Craig Reid had also only been on the planet for 17 years and 36 days when lining up against the English in 1881, but as he had lived through an extra leap year the sticklers who compile the International Rugby Yearbook decided to make him the second youngest.

LEFT 20 year old Jonah Lomu wreaking havoc on the England defence during the 1995 Rugby World Cup

RIGHT Samoan centre Brian 'the chiropractor' Lima is still practising his art in 2003, 14 years after his debut. South African halfback Derick Hougaard will testify to that

The magnificent Samoan centre Brian 'the chiropractor' Lima, now 32, was a mere 18 years and 66 days when first playing for his country. He was still re-arranging opposition bones at the 2003 World Cup.

That tournament was notable for the appearance of a number of young-sters. Georgian scrum-half Merab Kvirikashvili was 19 when he headed to Australia and there were about 10 players who were aged only 20, including Wales' Jonathan Thomas, Samoa's Sailosi Tagicakibau and the United States' flanker Todd Clever. Joe Rokocoko was also 20 as were Schalk Burger, the South African back rower, Frederic Michalak of France and Italy's Mirco Bergamasco. And proving that if you're good enough you're old enough, Thomas, Rokocoko and Michalak were three of the stand-out performers of the tournament.

The England women's team fielded their youngest player in 2003 when the Bath schoolgirl and scrum-half Danielle Waterman, 18, came on as a replacement for Susie Appleby in the Grand Slam-clinching game against Ireland in Limerick.

Young players also have the chance to shine on the international stage in their own age groups. The Under-19s World Cup was first played in 1969 and France won the inaugural tournament in Barcelona before going on to win the next two as well. In fact, the French have absolutely dominated the tournament, winning it 10 times in a row from 1974 before Italy broke their grip on the competition.

Many stars of the future cut their international teeth in the tournament, but sadly the 2004 tournament was marred by the death of the Irish flanker John McCall of heart failure during a match against New Zealand. The Ireland team withdrew as a mark of respect to this brilliant, much-missed prospect.

The Under-21s World Cup started in 1995 and saw the Junior All Blacks run out winners in the final of an event that has been dominated by the southern hemisphere sides. It is interesting to note that England, despite being a dominant force in senior international rugby, have a relatively poor record when it comes to the age-group events, even though many of their top players represented England at various stages before becoming international stars.

BELOW John McCall (left) of Ireland makes a tackle during the IRB U-19 World Championship match between New Zealand and Ireland played in Durban. McCall tragically collapsed and died of heart failure later in the game.

Zurich

FOR MORE THAN 100 YEARS ENGLISH rugby prospered without a league structure. The occasional cup competition came along but sides were happy with a series of hard-fought rivalries through friendlies. In 1987 that all changed with the establishment of the Courage Leagues.

These Courage Leagues developed when the title sponsorship was taken over by Allied Dunbar and in 2000 by Zurich, who established the top flight of English rugby as the Zurich Premiership.

At the birth of the English League structure two sides, Bath and Leicester, dominated proceedings. In the first ten years their domination was only broken twice, and both times by Wasps.

Clubs weren't that keen on giving up all their longstanding friendlies in those early years and for the first six seasons clubs in the top flight only

played each other once. The structure developed into the fixture list we see today where sides play every other side in the Zurich Premiership twice a season, home and away.

Leicester were England's first official champions, in 1988, led by 126 league points from Dusty Hare, taking the title from Wasps, with a win on the last day of the season against Waterloo.

The remarkable Hare, who scored 368 points in all matches in that season, recorded 20 in their final 39-15 victory.

Leicester's first title didn't lead to domination by the Midlands side and within a year there was a new name on the trophy, Bath.

Bath's 1989 crown kicked off an incredible domination of the English game by the men from The Recreation Ground. They won an almost unbelievable six titles in the next eight years. Wasps stopped their total domination in 1990 and there was a title for Leicester in 1995.

That 1989 title for Bath was accompanied by a Pilkington Cup Final victory, at Twickenham, against Leicester, presenting Bath with the first league and cup double.

The legendary Bath team of the late 1980s and early 1990s went on to complete seven cup final victories and four successive Courage League titles between 1991 and 1994. They dominated English rugby in the way Liverpool had done before them and Manchester United after them in football.

The first of two league and cup doubles arrived in the 1988-89 season when club legends such as John Palmer, Jeremy Guscott, Andy Robinson, Tony Swift, Stuart Barnes, Richard Hill, Graham Dawe, Gareth Chilcott and Nigel Redman proved how good they were.

The league title in 1989 was won with a 22-16 win over Nottingham, with two games to play. At Twickenham the double was completed with a 10-6 win over Leicester, in front of 58,000 fans, which was a world record for a club match.

The second double followed in 1992 when Stephen Jones, writing in The Sunday Times said: "Bath have the ability, when they need to, to rise to a different planet."

The arrival of professional rugby, in 1995, saw a new team come to the forefront of English rugby and after Bath and Wasps won titles in 1996 and 1997 it was Newcastle's turn, in 1998.

OPPOSITE Dusty Hare runs with the ball in the 1988 Courage League decider against Waterloo

BELOW Bath celebrate their fourth consecutive Courage League title in 1994

Newcastle, coached by former England outside-half Rob Andrew, won their lone title by one point from Saracens, in a season when Samoan Pat Lam confirmed his status as one of the legends of the game.

Newcastle also became the only side to win the Championship in their first season after promotion.

Leicester handled the initial move to professionalism better than any other side in the Northern Hemisphere, reigning supreme in England and Europe, matching Bath's feat of winning four successive English titles.

Before the game turned professional Leicester battled for supremacy with Bath but once the Tigers had won their first English title, in 1999 they were unstoppable. They completed an incredible four consecutive English championship victories, starting in 1999, and lifted back-to-back Heineken cups in 2001 and 2002.

Coached by Dean Richards and John Wells, in those four years of dominance, Leicester were almost unbeatable. They went 57 home matches undefeated in the Premiership between 30 December 1997 and 30 November 2002, when Northampton beat them. Their incredible run included 52 successive wins.

Captained by Martin Johnson (See J for Johnno, Jason and Jonny) for all four of their titles, they lost only 14 of the 92 Premiership matches they played over those four championship-winning seasons.

In claiming that last title - in 2002 - Leicester had it almost won by Christmas, such was their domination.

They lost just four times, scored more tries (72) than any other side and, significantly, conceded just 19 tries, 17 less than the next best, Northampton.

Chief Executive Peter Wheeler, a former club player, summed up the philosophy that underpinned their success. He said: "Nothing is taken for granted. We have no divine right to success.

"There's a good work ethic here, a self-critical attitude too. Complacency isn't tolerated. No one will tell you how good you are, only how to get better. We've never been a club to pat itself on the back.

"If you stand still then you're history."

The four titles weren't the first the first time Leicester moved into the history books as they won three consecutive English Cup finals from 1979 to 1981.

In between Bath and Leicester's triumphs Wasps were the best team in England three times. In 2003 they lifted the trophy at the end of a new play-off system.

From 2003 the top three sides at the end of the regular season go into a play-off. Second plays third, the winner taking on the side that came first, in a Twickenham Grand Final.

In 2003 this pitted the league winners

ABOVE Worcester celebrate promotion to the Zurich Premiership having beaten Bristol Shoguns at Sixways on 3 April 2004

Gloucester against second-placed Wasps, captained by Lawrence Dallaglio.

The new system suited Wasps far better than Gloucester, who headed the league by 15 points, as the Wasps built up a momentum towards the end of the season to take the final game, at Twickenham, 39-3.

Promotion and relegation from National One was established in the 2002-03 season, after many years of wrangling, when Bristol were relegated and replaced by Rotherham.

Rotherham's stay in the Zurich Premiership lasted just 12 months when they were relegated, to be replaced in the top flight for the 2004-5 season by Worcester.

Bibliography:

International Rugby Yearbook 2003-4, by Mick Cleary and John Griffiths

Men in Black by Ron Palenski and others

A History of Rugby - Marks and Spencer

The Daily Telegraph Chronicle of Rugby - Norman Barrett

Springbok Rugby, an Illustrated History - Chris Greyvenstein

The Australian Rugby Companion - Gordon Bray

Jeremy Guscott, The Autobiography

Bath, Ace of Clubs - Brian Jones

Rugby World Cup Sevens: Divine Intervention - John Blondin

Wallaby Gold - Peter Jenkins and Matthew Alvarez

The Complete Guide to Rugby Union - Richard Bath

The Encyclopedia of New Zealand Rugby - Rod Chester and others

Australian Rugby - The Game and The Players - Jack Pollard

The Carling Years - Mick Cleary

The Book of English International Rugby - John Griffiths

Rugby and All That - Martin Johnson

Midnight Rugby - Stephen Jones

Martin Johnson, the autobiography - Martin Johnson

Jason Leonard, the autobiography - Jason Leonard and Alison Kervin

Decade of the Dragon, John Taylor

www.rugbyworld.com

www.rugby.com.au

www.sru.org.uk

www.rfu.com

www.planet-rugby.com

The pictures in this book were provided courtesy of the following:

GETTY IMAGES
101 Bayham Street, London NW1 0AG

COLORSPORT
The Courtyard, Lynton Road, London N8 8SL

MUSEUM OF RUGBY, TWICKENHAM
Rugby Road, Twickenham TW1 1DS

Book design and artwork by Darren Roberts

Published by Green Umbrella

Series Editors Jules Gammond and Tim Exell

Written by Paul Morgan and Adam Hathaway

With thanks to Rugby World

Rugby World is the world's best-selling rugby magazine. To keep up to date
with the rugby world see www.rugbyworld.com